Life Is Love, Enjoy It!

by Joy Thomas

ONTIC BOOK PUBLISHERS
P. O. Box 3291
Beaumont, California 92223
U.S.A.

ISBN 0-9624494-3-1

Printed in the United States of America

DISTRIBUTED BY
SATHYA SAI BOOK CENTER
OF AMERICA
305 W. FIRST ST
TUSTIN, CA 92680, USA

With eternal devotion

to

Our Beloved Savior and Lord

Sathya Sai Baba

BOOKS BY THE SAME AUTHOR

Life Is a Game, Play It!
Life Is a Challenge, Meet It!
Life Is a Dream, Realize It!

ACKNOWLEDGMENTS

With deep gratitude to Sathya Sai Baba, Raye and I acknowledge His expressions Betty and David Davidson, Mahri and Bruce Kintz, Crystal Pearl, Susan Jansen, Joan Davies, Peggy Gillian Wood, and Diane Wells. Each person mentioned within the pages of this book, and many who are not, played the role assigned to him or her with the utmost skill and compassion and we hereby express our gratitude and our love. We also wish to acknowledge Baba's photographers to whom we are indebted for the beautiful pictures.

INTRODUCTION

When my husband, Raye, and I first heard the name of Sri Sathya Sai Baba in 1981, we knew that, by some miracle, we had been given the maximum grace which could be won in a lifetime. Our first visit to Him confirmed and strengthened this conviction. Now, thirteen years later, we look back on an unprecedented acceleration of our spiritual evolution with undying gratitude to Him for His patience and love. He is always with each one who chooses to call on Him, wherever they may be, and to be in His presence is to be conscious of divine grace here and now.

Some have heard of Him but have felt unworthy to approach. To those I wish to say that Raye and I are very ordinary mortals. Our names do not appear in most of the prestigious categories in which we humans place each other. We were both born into working class families in the southern part of the United States. Both of us had the blessing of being born to loving parents, who gave us a firm grounding in duty, morality, and service to others, but neither of us have ever at any time held any claim to wealth, aristocratic forefathers, fame, or unusual accomplishments. The fact that Bhagavan Sri Sathya Sai Baba has seen fit to receive us into His private interview room, to speak to us in darshan, and to accept and bless the books we have worked together to produce, is certainly proof positive that He loves each of us only for the Divine spark within us. No one is classified by Him as unworthy. He has said, "Take one step toward me, and I will take one hundred toward you." That one step is all that is required.

In each of our first three books about Sathya Sai Baba, He was quoted as recorded in **Sai Avatar, Vol. II,** as follows:

> *The wise man is he who keeps his reason sharp and clear and sees things as they really are. He listens to this advice:*
>
> *Life is a challenge, meet it.*
Life is Love, share it.
Life is a dream, realize it.
Life is a game, play it.
>
> *This is the real pilgrim's progress. This is the lion's march across the forest--fearless, masterful, and victorious.*

--Bhagavan Sri Sathya Sai Baba

It gives me immense joy that He has allowed me to write a series of four books, using each of these statements as a title. **Life Is a Game, Play It!** came first, followed by **Life Is a Challenge, Meet It!** and **Life is a Dream, Realize It!** In an interview at Sai's ashram, Prasanthi Nilayam in Puttaparthi, Andhra Pradesh, India, in 1989, following the publication of **Life Is a Game,** He told me to get started on another book. In naming the remaining three, He said, "Life is love, live it!" However, on other occasions, He has been heard to say, "Life is love, enjoy it!" Therefore, in an interview with Him on February 1, 1993, I asked Him, "Swami, you have said, 'Life is Love, share it,' 'Life is Love, live it,' and Life is Love, enjoy it.' Which should be the name of the fourth book?" He responded quickly and emphatically, "Life is Love, enjoy it!"

And, indeed, His injunction to "Be happy!" is well known to His devotees. He has assured us that He, Himself, is always happy, even though He must occasionally pretend to frown and scold in order that we will recognize and refrain from the behaviors which slow us down on our spiritual journey. This drama, which we call life, was never intended to be an ordeal, but when we take on a role in the play and lose ourselves in the part, we experience the conflicts, the trials, and the tribulations which are necessary to carry out the plot. When we are content to sit in the audience and be a detached observer, the play is pure joy.

It is, therefore, the intention of this book to describe experiences which have provided individualized instruction in how to enjoy life, how to expand Love, how to meet challenges, and how to increase Wisdom, validating each through the teachings of our beloved Swami, the Avatar to this age.

--The Author

I asked for strength, and God gave me difficulties to overcome.

I asked for wisdom, God gave me problems to learn to solve.

I asked for prosperity, God gave me the brain and brawn to work.

I asked for courage, and God gave me dangers to overcome.

I asked for Love, and God gave me troubled people to help.

I asked for favors, and God gave me opportunities.

I received nothing--nothing I wanted.

I received everything--everything I needed.

My prayer was answered.

--Author Unknown

TABLE OF CONTENTS

Chapter One

THE END OF KNOWLEDGE IS LOVE

On my first trip to India, had anyone asked me why I was going, I would certainly have replied that I was looking for a living Master. However, if the questioner had pursued his inquiry further, I would have undoubtedly admitted that I wanted knowledge. I had heard many different theories about the purpose of life, but I wanted someone who really knew the answer to explain it to me. Who am I? Why am I here? How was I created? What am I supposed to do? In short, what is this thing we call life all about?

Looking back, I doubt very seriously that I would have said that I wanted to learn more about Love, although I accepted Love as a synonym for God. However, in the first interview which He granted me, Sathya Sai, my true mother, began the instruction which He knew to be essential to my spiritual growth. On December 16, 1981, He asked, "How many children do you have?" When I replied, "Two, Swami," He corrected me, saying, "You have seven children." As He declined to elaborate further on His statement, I was left to ponder it on my own.

It took five years of praying, seeking, yearning, studying, inquiring, before the meaning of Swami's saying was revealed to me. Glancing through a friend's copy of **The Aquarian Gospel of Jesus, the Christ,** I read "Seven is the number of the all, including every man." This "accidental" discovery was accepted immediately. I knew that Swami taught His devotees to love all, but I just hadn't realized that it was the message He had specifically directed to me.

So, now I knew, but could I obey? I wrote to Him, asking that He teach me to love, and I made earnest efforts. At times I felt I was succeeding. At other times, it seemed that I was as unloving as ever. Then there were periods in which expanding my ability to love seemed less important than other character improvements which I was striving to make.

It was in Kodaikanal in April, 1992, that the subject was brought up again by my beloved Lord. Standing on the balcony, looking down at me on the ground below, He asked, "How many children do you have?" Startled at the question, and still not firmly grounded in the expanded sense of love for which Baba was looking, I replied, "Two, Swami." He either feigned great surprise or threw up His hands in despair, I'm not quite sure which, and asked with emphasis on the first syllable and elongation of both words, "Only two?"

Of course, this time it didn't take me five years to figure out what he meant. I was instantly aware of what I had done and why. Obviously, my attempts to love more had not become imbedded at the feeling level, and, when asked for a spontaneous response, I still could only claim to love two people completely and unconditionally. Knowing Swami as I have now for a number of years, I knew that He was not trying to trip me up or punish me. He was only showing me to myself in a way which could not be denied, in a way which left me no choice. If I truly wanted what I said I wanted--liberation from the attachments and illusions of the world--then I would have to stop trying and start doing.

From that moment, I made it a priority to feel love for all. By visualizing each one as Swami's child, as a spark of the Divine, I began to really change. It wasn't at all difficult to love other Baba devotees, to love my nice and friendly neighbors, but to love those who were not friendly to me, who waged war on others, who destroyed lives and homes, who contaminated the planet, or who attempted to undermine the dharmic efforts of others--that took some doing. At first, I had to imagine each of them as being my own child. I had to feel the love that I generously bestow on my own son and daughter without regard for their actions, then expand that love to include the specific group whose behavior was threatening to make me feel less than loving toward them.

In performing this exercise, I learned many things. On one occasion, I was struggling very hard to love one group which was causing pain and suffering to people whom I classified as innocent victims. I was able to succeed in my effort. Some months later, however, those who had been the victims became the aggressors, and the entire situation was reversed. I was so grateful that I had been able to see them all as God's children, thus not needing to change any allegiance I might have felt toward the side "in the right."

For those of you who may be striving to overcome criticism and condemnation of others, let me encourage you to continue. You will win the battle, and you will be happier than you ever dreamed you could be. At first, you may slip back into the old habits from time to time, but don't let that stop you. Remember that all are as close to you and as dear to you as your children. We are all the children of the One Father, an inseparable family unit. Love all, including yourself.

It was on February 1, 1993, that I was sitting on Swami's left side in the interview room at Puttaparthi. After speaking to someone on His right, He turned to me suddenly and asked, "How many children do you have?" Again I found myself under the stress of circumstances to answer Him quickly. I placed my hand on my heart and replied, "All are my children, Swami." His face lit up in that most wonderful smile, pure love streaming out of the crystalline heart of God. He turned to the group and joyously exclaimed, "She got it right! She got it right!"

In only a minute or two, you have read the story of the lessons which came to this devotee after she had prayed to Bhagavan Sri Sathya Sai Baba to teach her to love. These lessons were, however, spread out over a period of twelve years, many of them involving tremendous struggles on the part of the learner. If you would like to gain a better perspective on Baba's teaching methods, or look at the situations in greater detail, you may read or reread the following:

The prayer asking Swami to teach me to love: **Game**, p. 65.

He tells me, "You Have Seven Children": **Game**, pp. 66-74.

Loving those who seem not to love you: **Challenge**, pp. 93-112.

Swami removes hate from my heart: **Dream**, pp. 51-58.

There are no differences among God's children: **Dream**, pp. 59-64.

I flunk the test again: **Dream**, pp. 85-89.
Loving all: **Dream**, pp. 97-104, 113-118.

* * * * * * * * *

God has incarnated in human form in order to inspire man to follow higher ideals—not only in India but in foreign countries also. Men may have different languages and lifestyles, but God is One and He is present everywhere. All religions speak of Him as Love and as attainable through Love. Forms of worshiping God differ for they are based by time and place, but Love is the basic content of all the forms. The language of Love is understood and spoken by all hearts. There is only one race really, and that is the race of mankind. We now consider petty distinctions of nationality, race, religion, and language as vital and hold back the Love which must flow to everyone from the heart. That was the life and message of Jesus. Nurture it in your hearts. Experience Jesus as your Messenger sent from God.

Love alone can reveal the Divinity latent in all. Love is God. Live in Love. Love lives by giving and forgiving; self lives by getting and forgetting. Love is selflessness; selfishness is Lovelessness. Do not waste your life pursuing the narrow interests of the self. Love! Love! Become what you truly are—the embodiments of Love. No matter how others treat you or what they think of you, do not worry. Follow Jesus Christ. Love for the sake of your own evolution and not for what others say.... Your own heart shining with Love is God's Love.... You should constantly remind yourself, "I am God," "I am God," "I am God." The day you see yourself as God you become God.

--Bhagavan Sri Sathya Sai Baba
Sathya Sai Speaks, Vol. 11, pp. 14-15

Chapter Two

CARING IS LOVE

During the years in which Swami was patiently teaching me to love, He showered Raye with His love, frequently commenting on Raye's loving ways. For example, He has told me more than once, "He [Raye] takes such good care of you."

Raye's life has been characterized by caring from his youth. Before we were married, I asked him what he remembered as the happiest event of his childhood. I must have thought he would tell me about a birthday party, a special Christmas gift, or something that someone had done for him. His actual response was quite different. He told of his own family and their neighbors working very hard just to keep food on their tables and to buy fuel for their stoves and lamps. One day when Raye was about seven years old, his father had been able to earn some extra money and had brought home several jugs of coal oil, which was used in the lamps which lighted the house. As the sun disappeared over the horizon and darkness surrounded the little cabins, they noticed that their neighbor's home remained dark. Raye's father handed him one of the jugs of coal oil and told him to take it to the neighbor. Raye crossed the fields which separated the two homes, gave the coal oil to the neighbor, and started back across the fields. He said that when he looked back and saw the light shining from the window of the neighbor's house, he felt so happy that he still remembers it as one of the happiest moments of his early years.

To make someone else happy is still Raye's greatest satisfaction. When Swami called our group for interview on February 1, 1993, Raye removed his big ring and put it in his pocket. Swami has spoken of it and blessed it on several occasions. In one interview He took the ring from Raye, held it up for the group to see, and then pointed to each of the enameled pictures in turn, saying, "This is Shirdi, this is Om, this is Jesus, and this is me!" Raye did not want to take any of Swami's time or attention from others in the group who had questions that they felt they urgently needed to ask. As so many of us have learned, however, you can't secondguess Swami or manipulate His actions in any way. One of the first questions Swami asked in the outer interview room was directed to Raye. "Where is the big ring?" He asked, as if He didn't know.

Raye attempted to extricate it from his pocket, but Swami said, "Nevermind, just give me "Nine Diamonds." ("Nine Diamonds" is the name Swami gave to the nine gem ring which he manifested for Raye several years ago.) Raye then removed the nine gem ring from his finger and gave it to Swami. Baba showed it to the group and then waved His hand. Instantly the nine gem ring was dematerialized, and a very large diamond ring in a gold setting appeared. Again, Swami showed the big diamond to the group. Then he took Raye's left hand in His and attempted to put the ring on his ring finger. Swami pushed, seemingly exerting considerable force, but the ring would not go over the knuckle.

Raye began then to try to put the ring on his finger. He pushed, twisted, and strained, but the ring would not go over the second joint. After Raye had exhausted all of the methods he could think of, Swami told him to just leave it as it was. Thus, when we were called into the inner interview room, the strikingly beautiful big diamond rested between the first and second joints of Raye's ring finger.

When the group was settled down inside, Raye was seated on Swami's right hand and, due to the loving generosity of the group members, the seat on Swami's left had been saved for me. Swami then asked Raye for the ring. Holding it in His hand, He looked at me and said, "Which do you like, big diamond or nine diamonds?" Without volition on my part, the words, "Nine diamonds, Swami," came from my mouth. Swami looked at Raye, then, and said, "Oooooh, wife likes nine diamonds." Then he blew on the big diamond and it disappeared into the ether as the nine gem ring reappeared. When He replaced the ring on Raye's finger, it slipped on easily. When we had left home, the ring had been quite tight and Raye had made the statement that, if he got the chance, he might ask Swami to make his nine gem ring a little larger. Of course, he had never asked, but Swami knew what he wanted, and He made the nine gem ring fit perfectly.

Picture of the big ring: **Challenge**, p. 152d.
Baba's blessing of big ring: **Challenge**, p. 160.
Manifestation of the nine gem ring: **Game** pp. 174-179.

* * * * * * * * *

DIAMOND: Enhances brain functions. Aids alignment of cranial bones. Breaks up blockages in crown chakra and in the personality. Master healer. Dispels negativity. Purifies physical/etheric bodies. Reflects will and power aspects of God. Enhances full spectrum of energies in body/mind/spirit. Alignment with Higher Self. Abundance, innocence, purity, faithfulness, all chakras.

--Crystal Awareness Guide from Legion of Light

Chapter Three

SEEING THE ROPE AS A SNAKE

After returning to the United States, we resumed our customary activities. There were weekly and monthly devotional meetings of the Sathya Sai Baba Center of Cherry Valley being held in our home. Raye worked at his customary activities of serving home buyers and sellers. I did a little reading, a little writing, held twice-weekly satsangs, and occasionally had the opportunity to be of some slight service to a fellow being. Our life was comfortable and, we thought, secure.

It was in May, 1993, that the first slight rumble was heard in this otherwise quiet and peaceful existence. Raye came home one day and, with a very puzzled look on his face, said, "Something seems to be wrong, but I don't know what it is." My questions managed to narrow this problem down to something relating to his body, but otherwise he was not able to tell me anything more. He didn't have any specific pain. Everything seemed to be functioning normally. Something just felt wrong.

A couple of weeks later he complained that his left foot was extremely cold most of the time, but sometimes it would warm up suddenly and the heat would increase to the point of burning. The first week in June, while he was showing a house, he accidentally bumped into a coffee table, lost his balance and took a slight fall. When he came home, he showed me a large black and blue lump on his left shin. It did not seem too surprising that his left leg was quite painful.

As the pain continued to grow worse, it seemed wise to have it checked. X-rays were taken. They showed nothing, but the pain continued. Looking for the source of the pain, the doctors ordered a bone scan. Again, nothing appeared which would cause the extreme discomfort. Surprisingly, the right foot and leg became involved. The alternating heat and cold affected the right foot as well as the left, and the pain was felt now in both legs.

Over the next few weeks, the severity of the pain increased and it was being felt in the lower back as well as the legs. At this point, both Raye and I began to feel that the source of the problem had been the back from the beginning. Twenty years ago Raye had been in an industrial accident which crushed two disks in his back. At that time, he had been cautioned not to lift, to do certain exercises, and to take care not to place any strain on his back. He had never had any pain which was as intense as that which he was experiencing now, but he had suffered from leg pains or sciatica which was due to the back injury.

So, when given this new insight, the doctors ordered a CT Scan of the lower back. The result showed evidence of the former injury, of course, and indicated some pressure on a nerve, but nothing was found that would cause the unbearable pain which went on now day and night. The doctors were mystified. One suggested elastic stockings, another thought long walks might be the answer, and one intimated that Raye must be making the whole thing up since there was no physical cause for his distress.

As the pain continued unabated, sleep became more and more impossible. Even though painkillers and sleeping aids did not work, they were the only medical aids that held out any hope at all. Raye took them in desperation.

Then a new phenomenon surfaced. Along with the deathly coldness of the feet, we noticed a darkening of the toenails. They looked as if they had been badly mashed. The color ranged from deep red to dark brown. We again hoped that this might provide the doctors with a clue to whatever was going on. They said, "Ah, a circulation problem!" But, again, tests proved conclusively that there was no problem with Raye's circulation. Once more our hopes for a medical solution were dashed.

Dear friends, who wanted so much to help, referred us to highly respected chiropractors, herbalists, acupuncturists, homeopaths, and neurosurgeons. We followed up every lead, but there seemed to be no answer to be found in any type of medical or manipulative procedure.

Both of us were praying to Swami for His help. I sent a cablegram to Him, prayed day and night, and chanted the Gayatri. Raye would lie on the floor at the foot of the chair which is reserved for Baba in our living room, talking to Him and begging for His help for hours at a time. I sent letters with a number of devotees, pleading with Baba to heal Raye and to help us understand what was going on. However, months passed and Swami did not send any message that could be specifically related to that little Form in India. It seemed to us that if we were to have any word from Baba, we would have to go to India to get it.

Even though it seemed like a wild idea, nothing else was working, and so we went ahead with arrangements to go to India. We stocked up on the strongest painkillers and bought our tickets, but it was not to be. Before time to leave, Raye's pain was so great, and he had been for so long without sleep, that he overdosed on the pain pills. On the morning of November 2, 1993, Raye was taken to the emergency room of our local hospital at 7:00 a.m. At 10:00 a.m. I was told that I would have to evacuate our house, taking whatever I could gather up in ten minutes. There were fires on the hillsides surrounding us, and high winds were driving the flames rapidly towards our little community.

I took a file labeled "Legal Records," a few clothes, Baba's robe, and the little statue of Ganapathi which Baba had manifested for me in Brindavan in 1990. Everything else which we called our possessions were left behind. I felt a complete release of attachment to these things, including the house. As I closed the door behind me, I said, "Baba, the house is Yours, the Center is Yours, everything here is Yours. Whatever is Your will, I accept."

It was only later that I came across Swami's reference to those of us who claim that we have surrendered to him, saying that, in effect, we were only deluding ourselves. I did genuinely release all of our possessions, but to have said that I accepted whatever was His will was an exaggeration. Even though I had quoted from my early religious teachings, "All that is, is the will of God, and all is good," I was having extreme difficulty accepting that the agony of my dearly beloved husband was either God's will or good.

Being unable to get a direct communication from Swami, I spoke to Him in the way I customarily do. Almost daily, I ask Him for a message, open a book He has written or one of discourses He has given. It has almost never failed to have given me exactly what I need at the moment. So, I asked Him the question **WHAT IS HAPPENING?** and, selecting a book and opening it at random, I read His words:

> *When the Cosmos manifested through the will of God, Who is the Universal Absolute, It arose from the Absolute only, since there was then only ONE, just as even now there is only ONE, despite all this seeming variety. That Will which emanated from the Absolute persuaded us to see and experience Many; that is all that has happened. The One Reality is still the One; It has not undergone any change. It is we who have superimposed the illusion of Many on the One.*

Then I asked **WHAT IS THE ILLUSION?** and selecting randomly again, I read:

> *When you feel you are an individual, you are separated from God; when you feel that you are divine, you are One with Him. Seeing the rope as a snake makes you shiver; seeing it as the rope, you lose fear. The snake did not arrive*

or depart; the rope did not arrive or depart. Light appeared and darkness disappeared. Ignorance fled and knowledge dawned.

But, Swami, I asked **DOES THE ILLUSION HAVE TO BE SO PAINFUL?** and the answer came:

You proceed from death to life and from illness to health by the experience of the buffetings of the world. The world is a very essential part of the curriculum of man; through loss of peace—even agony—an infant is born. The pains are worthwhile; they precede the birth of new life.... Paramatma draws the jivatma towards itself. It is the nature of both to have this affinity, for they are the same. They are like the iron and the magnet. But if the iron is rusty, the magnet is unable to attract. Remove the impediment; that is all you have to do. Shine forth in your real nature, and the Lord will draw you into His bosom. Trials and tribulations are the means through which this cleansing is done.

All right then, Swami, tell me what to do. I feel so helpless. You must know how difficult it is to watch a loved one suffer. **WHAT CAN I DO?** When I opened the book which came to my hand, the words I read were these:

When obstacles come (either in your experience or the experience of others), meet them with courage. They harden you; they make you tough. The best way to get rid of weakness is to strike at the very taproot of the tree—the mistake that you (or they) are the body, with this name, this form, these senses, this intelligence, and this mind. These are all the luggage you carry. Don't you say, "my nose, my mind, my hand, my reason," just as you say, "my book, my umbrella"? Who is this "I" that calls all these "mine"? It is the real "you." It was there when you were born, when you were sleeping forgetful of all else, forgetful even of your body and its equipment, internal and external. That "I" cannot be harmed; it does not change; it knows no death or birth. Learn the discipline that makes you aware of this Truth.

At the time these quotations were given me, their source was of no importance at all. I regret now that I cannot tell you from which books they were taken, as I wrote them for my own use only. Looking over them again, as I now write them to share with you, I am in awe at their pertinence. Could Swami have answered the questions any better in person? Could He have sat down and written this all out in His precious handwriting, sent it to me in the mail or with another devotee, and given me better answers than these? His personal attention would have given me bliss, but He has infinite resources with which to teach and assist His devotees. He uses the methods which are particularly appropriate for each individual. He answered my prayers for His guidance through words on the printed pages of His books. I can hear His voice so clearly in my memory as it sounded when He told Raye, looking at me with an indulgent smile, "She loves words!" So, I thank you, Swami, for the words. They helped me make it through the severest trial which I have had during this incarnation.

* * * * * * * * *

When you intend going on a journey, you hand over the keys of the car to the chauffeur and sit in comfort and security in the back seat, forgetting the possible trouble on the way. You have surrendered your life into the hands of this man, his intelligence, alertness, and skill. Some men do not fully surrender; they are too egoistic for that. They interrupt him every minute with tips, hints and suggestions about driving, questions and doubts regarding the condition of the car or the road. And, lo, they confuse him and confound his confidence, so much so that they inflict accidents upon themselves. Be steady, have faith, and reach the goal safely. Life is the car, your heart is the key, God is the chauffeur. Surrender to Him and be rid of further bother. Travel safely and arrive happily.

There are many who declare that they have surrendered to me. They have dedicated their all, they proclaim. But they still continue with their 'I did it,' I feel so,' 'I think so,' 'I like it.' 'I do not like it,' etc. The 'I' raises its hood in order that it may receive homage or praise! Now! It is a big lie to say that you have surrendered! It is sheer falsehood. The word surrender is a word that is just thrown about without any value or purpose, to deceive people who do not dive into its authenticity. How can you surrender something over which you have no control? You are the slave of your mind, of your passions, of your prejudices; yet, you dare claim that you have surrendered your mind, your thoughts, your plans, to God! While you are struggling to escape from the coils of the mind and the stranglehold of the passions, how can you dedicate them to me? No. You need not boast of such bravery, such sacrifice, such devotion. I do not need or ask for such declaration. It is enough if you believe that God is everywhere and at all times and that you are no different from Him. When you are God yourself, to whom are you to surrender what? Think this over deeply and attain to this realization.

--Baba
Sathya Sai Speaks, Vol. VII, Chap. 79, pp. 464-5

A rope might appear as many things; it might provoke various feelings and reactions in various people...but it never changes into many; it is ever One.... Reason and discriminate; then believe and experience.

--Baba
Geetha Vahini, Chapter 12
American Translation by David Davidson

Sai Baba of Shirdi

Chapter Four

COURAGEOUS PATIENCE NEEDED

You may be wondering whether our house burned or not. No, due to the heroic efforts of many professional firefighters and brave volunteers, the fire was stopped after it had destroyed only four homes. Ours was untouched, and twelve hours after I had been told to evacuate, I was allowed to return. Due to a shortage of water, the fire had been allowed to come very close to the residential community before any attempt was made to put it out. The circumstances reminded me of many other last-minute reprieves I had received since becoming a Baba devotee. These are so common that, among ourselves, devotees refer to their beloved Baba as "Last-Minute Sai."

Now one fire was out. My house was out of danger, but my husband was not. After his release from the hospital, he began to express irrational fears of being harmed. His outlook had deteriorated to the point that he held out no hope for his survival. He was still in constant pain, still unable to sleep, and his mental state grew worse by the day. He overdosed for the second time. This time his hospitalization was lengthier. I found myself alone except for the one hour each day when I was allowed to visit.

I continued my struggle to surrender, accept, and trust, but failure seemed to occur more often than success. I went over and over all the things I knew that should be of some comfort to me. According to the Vedas (Hindu scriptures), there are four Yugas or ages of creation. These move in a circular sequence. When the last is finished, the cycle begins again. At the very bottom of the cycle is the Kali Yuga, the age in which we are at the present time. For those whose goals are happiness and success in worldly matters, it is of all ages the most difficult. However, for those who desire eternal bliss in union with God, it is of all ages the most conducive to liberation from the endless cycle of birth and death. Did I just want a comfortable life with a healthy, loving husband at my side, or did I really desire that both of us be liberated?

The Kali Yuga is characterized by man's inhumanity to man, by lack of satisfaction in human endeavors, lack of fulfillment in human relationships, and the proliferation of financial and physical ills. Raye and I have certainly experienced most of these pains and frustrations, as have many others of our acquaintance. Should we not now focus all of our efforts on gaining that which is most readily available in these trying times: liberation?

Raye and I are both students of the Bible and the Vedas, and we have been given the incredible grace to have visited Bhagavan Sri Sathya Sai Baba, the Avatar to this age, on numerous occasions. His Love is all-pervading, ever-comforting, and grace-conferring, and He encourages us to use our power of discrimination and to strengthen our spiritual convictions through our own efforts. It was only natural that, in our time of trial, we would turn with renewed vigor to the study of His teachings.

Some readers may not know that Sathya Sai is the second incarnation of this Avatar, the first embodiment having been referred to as Shirdi Sai. An Avatar is one who voluntarily comes in human form, though having much greater than human power and wisdom, for the purpose of helping others to free themselves from the bondage to birth and death. Though I revere and adore Sathya Sai Baba, I had never taken any interest in Shirdi Sai Baba, though His teachings are readily available in book form.

Now, finding myself overwhelmed by the number and intensity of problems facing me, I began to become acquainted with Shirdi for the first time. In the past I had never been able to work up any interest in Him at all, feeling that when He is right here in his Sathya Form, why should I bother with the funny old man that He was in His previous incarnation? As I stewed over the difficulties, tragedies, and disappointments which so many of the genuine seekers for Truth seem to be having today, somehow Shirdi seemed to be there to comfort me in my longing to understand. A friend had brought **Sri Sai Baba's Charters and Sayings** by H. H. Narasimha back from India. She quoted one of the sayings of Shirdi which was recorded in it: "I take away everything when I wish to show my favor." I felt that everything had been taken away from Raye and from me. Was it possible that these experiences which seemed so catastrophic could actually be a sign of the Lord's favor? My rational mind shouted, "No!" but somewhere deep inside my heart there was a flame of hope. Maybe God still loves us. Maybe He hasn't deserted us. Maybe, as impossible as it seems right now, we will eventually learn that something good has been going on all the time. I can say, "Everything is a sign of His grace," but can I really know it to the extent that I can completely accept whatever happens with no resistance at all?

Praying that I might find more strength to exercise the discipline of surrender, I asked my friend if I might borrow her book about Shirdi Sai. After what seemed ages to me, my friend finally brought it. She had been unable to locate the reference she had quoted to me, so I had no choice but to begin at the beginning. I read along, feeling more and more love coming from this dear old curmudgeon. I saw Him as the purveyor of "tough love," which many of us certainly need. We don't need to be cuddled and comforted in our ignorance; we need to be jolted out of it! I realized that, not only did Shirdi do that on a regular basis, but also that Our Beloved and Loving Sathya Sai is doing it now more and more. We have been asleep and dreaming long enough; it's time now to wake up, throw off the vasanas (old thought patterns), and open the windows to let the light stream in.

I was grateful to read and to believe that all that is going on is the Grace of Sai and all is good, but how could I internalize that? How could I make it a part of my being? One of the things that I had never understood about Shirdi Sai was that he was constantly asking his devotees for money (dakshina). Our Sathya Sai does not ask for donations of any kind, so why did Shirdi? I began reading the section on dakshina in **Sri Sai Baba's Charters and Sayings** with some resistance. The definition of dakshina, on page 90, is stated as "a means of denuding a devotee of everything." It seemed very clear to me that he meant "everything that stands in the way of achieving liberation." Surely, Raye and I are both willing to have those things taken away which stand in the way of our liberation, aren't we?

Then, on page 91, I read, "Baba never takes except to give back tenfold." Then a number of stories are related of those who came to Shirdi Sai and gave Him everything they had, only to find that it all came back to them and more. Didn't Jesus say (Luke 6:38) "Give, and it shall be given unto you; good measure, pressed down, and shaken together, and running over, shall men give into your bosom. For with the same measure that ye mete withal, it shall be measured to you again"?

Have we not heard our own Sathya Sai say that we must all earn three zeros? We must first give up all possessions, then all family and friends, and finally we must willingly give up even our own good reputation. The information has always been available to me, but to give, or give up, in theory is easy. When it becomes specific, we are placed under the stress of circumstances to live up to those things we profess to believe. It became clear to me that giving money was the easiest of all giving. When Shirdi Baba asked for rupees, He only made renunciation sound easy. On page 95, the story is told of Shirdi asking one devotee for four guineas. Accepting the four guineas which the devotee promptly presented, He said, "But I have only one." The author says, "The obvious interpretation is that, though the devotee surrenders his fourfold Antahkarana (Manas [mind], Buddhi [intellect], Ahamkara [ego], and Chitta [consciousness]), Baba receives only the Jiva (individualized soul); all multiplicity, when it reaches God, becomes one. So the mind must surrender multiplicity unto the God Guru to attain unity." On page 96, Shirdi Baba is quoted as saying, "It is not these coins that I want. I want (1) faith and (2) patient endurance and waiting courageously). Give me these." Then a husband tells his wife (when Baba asks for six rupees), "Baba wants only your six inner enemies (lust, anger, greed, attachment, pride, and malice) to be surrendered to him." Then, on page 97, another devotee is quoted as saying, "You have not understood Baba. He cares not a rap for your rupees. What He wants is your mind and heart, your time and soul to be devoted to Him. That is His meaning."

And so it seems that if we surrender the mind, the intellect, the ego, and the heart willingly, all we get is the gold--tenfold. But when we hang on to our petty little attachments, He has to take them from us forceably. That's when the weeping and the gnashing of teeth occurs. When we surrender our family members to Him, He gives them back in a sense of perfect peace and unity. When we surrender our worldly goods, He demonstrates very clearly in our lives that He is bearing the burden of our welfare. As long as we resist, hang on, or pull back, there is pain. When we surrender, there is gain.

Shirdi said of His Guru (page 62), "By His Grace I attained to my present state. Making the Guru the sole object of one's thoughts and aims, one attains Paramartha, the Supreme Goal. This is the only truth the Guru taught me. The four sadhanas (spiritual exercises) and six sastras (regulations) are not necessary. **Trusting in the Guru fully is enough."**

Can we not accept the trials that come our way as the favor or Grace of God? Can we not surrender to His will without sniveling or fighting back? Can we not acknowledge that His desire for us is only good, and that the law of God is that none will fail? We will all someday wake up and realize ourselves to be God--perfect, happy, and fulfilled--and know that we have always been that. We must travel the razor's edge on which we acknowledge Him to be the doer, the director of the play, while we stand ready to carry out our roles to the last curtain. We must act, but only as His instruments. As Nisargadatta Maharaj said, "All you need doing is doing nothing. The doing happens. Trust me. I tell you that you are divine. Take it as the absolute truth. Your joy is divine. Your suffering is divine, too. All comes from God. Remember it always. You are God; your will alone is done."

And so we pray harder for the courageous patience to accept whatever He gives and to thank Him for His Love, whether it appears to us to result in either suffering or joy. This is not difficult if our goal is liberation from this dream of limitation and if the goal is kept constantly in view. Our attachments to health in our bodies, clarity in our minds, and wealth in our bank accounts, once surrendered to Him, will bring about evidence of His care in all aspects of our being and the peace that passeth all understanding.

* * * * * * * * *

Bear everything; do nothing.
Hear everything; say nothing.
Give everything; take nothing.
Serve everyone; be nothing.

--Sathya Sai Baba

"Bear All and Do Nothing"

Take a lesson from the sun, who shines his light on everyone
Or the rain that falls on every single shore.
No distinction of our race, or the color of our face,
Nature's gifts are there for all men rich or poor.

Love all, serve all.
Understand that love and peace is what we need.
Love all, serve all.
In every single thought, word, and deed.

Bear all and do nothing; hear all and say nothing,
Give all and take nothing in return.
Love is giving and forgiving, self is getting and forgetting,
Serve all in the spirit of pure love.

Love all, serve all.
Understand that love and peace is what we need.
Love all, serve all.
In every single thought, word, and deed.

--Bhajan on Australian Bhajan Tape

Chapter Five

THE DISCIPLINE OF SURRENDER

In the continuing struggle to surrender my will to His, I think I used every tool He has ever given us. I repeated His name. I chanted the Gayatri. I read, studied, and memorized His teachings. I played a tape of Hindu pundits chanting Sama Veda each night as I went to sleep. I could feel a calming of the agitated cells of my body as the sounds flowed over and through it. I repeated the Twenty-Third Psalm over and over, visualizing Baba as the gentle shepherd caring for and comforting his sheep. I reminded myself that He would make us lie down in green pastures and walk beside the still waters, even though we might not necessarily have chosen that ideal environment for our growth. Enforcing that thought, I read in Peggy Mason's Magazine, Winter, 1993, Baba's words: "There is only one freewill and that is God's will."

When I visited Raye, it was very difficult not to get caught up in the delusions from which he was suffering. He thought himself to be a forsaken and betrayed husband, and he had cast me in the role of the unfaithful wife. Each day as I left, I told him that I would be back to visit the next day. His standard answer was: "You won't need to come. I won't last that long. I'll be dead." The pain, from which there had not now been any relief for seven months, was no longer localized. When asked where he hurt, he would reply, "Everywhere."

In terms of our human circumstances, the quotation which helped me the most was:

Life is a newspaper. Read it in a casual manner--headlines, a few columns that catch your fancy, and throw it aside. Do not make it more important than that. Tomorrow it is waste paper. So, too, life is worth only a casual perusal. One birth is enough. Let the death coming to you be the last."

--Baba
Sathya Sai Speaks, Vol. VII, pp. 231-232

I had no desire whatsoever for additional reincarnations. When I had stated this prior to Raye's illness, he would always say, "Why not? You can always be of help to others." I wondered whether he still felt that way. Although I was more than willing not to be reborn, I had great difficulty releasing the desire to have this present incarnation run its course in a more peaceful manner than was presently the case. I read the following:

The fundamental factor in spiritual life is the suppression of desire: the surrender of the individual will to the Divine Will, which will elevate all thoughts, words, and deeds into acts of worship.

--Baba
Sathya Sai Speaks, Vol VI, Chap. 20, p. 98

I cannot claim to have ever completely surrendered to Baba or to have totally suppressed the desire for things to get better, but my efforts must have won His compassion. At last we received a message directly from Him. Bruce and Mahri Kintz had gone to India, carrying letters from Raye and me. They were aware of how much any response from Baba would mean to us. Thus it was that, when Baba came to Bruce and took the letter from him, Bruce asked, "Swami, do you have a message for Joy and Raye?" Swami did not reply, but immediately a candy fell into Bruce's lap. This was much more significant than it would have been had anyone offered candy for Baba to throw. There was no candy in evidence anywhere around except the one that dropped into Bruce's lap. He realized that the candy was Swami's answer to his question, and so he carefully saved it and brought it back to Raye. My own reaction to the candy came in a flash of understanding. I felt that Baba was telling us, "Even though this situation may seem bitter to you, you will ultimately realize it to be sweet."

Then we received a call from our dear friend and family doctor, Surya Reddy. He had done everything that allopathic medicine had to offer in his efforts to find some relief for Raye before he left for India. Then, putting his patient's needs before his own, when Swami stood before him in darshan, his first question was, "Swami, will you help Raye?" He said that Baba did not answer him in words, but He looked down at him with a smile that was at once comforting, as well as reassuring, and he felt confident that Swami not only knew all about what was going on with Raye, but that He was helping.

At about that same time, the first glimmer of light into the human situation came with a telephone call from Sharan Falotico of San Francisco. Many Sai Baba Center members worldwide, including those in the San Francisco Center had been regularly including Raye in their prayers to Swami. A devotee, whose profession was medical research, had called Sharan and asked her whether or not I knew that Raye's symptoms were, in his words, "those of classic kundalini arousal." When Sharan repeated the conversation to me, I was completely astounded. Being a natural student, I had read quite a few things about the kundalini over the past fifteen years, including Swami Muktananda's **The Play of Consciousness,** I. Bentov's **Stalking the Wild Pendulum,** R. Bucke's **Cosmic Consciousness,** and Leadbeater's several books on the subject. Yet the thought had not once occurred to me that Raye's experiences related to the kundalini in any way.

The thing that I remembered distinctly from what I had read was that "unwise practices," such as certain types of Pranayama (breath control) and overlong indulgence in meditation could bring about a premature kundalini arousal, sometimes causing mental problems. But Raye was not engaged in any such practices. Could this new information have any relevance at all? What does Baba say?

I recalled that our beloved Dr. Hislop had discussed the kundalini with Swami. In his book **Conversations** he had quoted Baba as having said that the kundalini did not exist, but in a letter dated July 6, 1990, he replied to a devotee who questioned the information by saying, "About kundalini--you did read [in my book] that the chakras do not exist, but in a second edition of **Conversations,** Baba had me remove that paragraph, saying that I had misunderstood Him.

"What Baba says is that it is not in any way necessary to work with or worry about the kundalini, that it will develop naturally and safely during the course of devotional sadhana.

"He also warns that work aimed at arousing the kundalini power is dangerous in the extreme, as are also the complex pranayama exercises. In the case of all of these systems, He says that no guru is alive today who himself achieved Self-Realization by the kundalini and pranayama disciplines taught by him, and the gurus are thus incapable of meeting unanticipated problems [arising from these practices]."

When I called Dr. Hislop to ask for permission to publish the above quotation from his letter, and asked what he thought might have caused Raye's difficulties, he suggested that it might have resulted from some action in a past life. This answer comforted me greatly.

The medical researcher from San Francisco had recommended that I read a book by B. S. Goel entitled **Third Eye and Kundalini.** Even though the book was published in India and not readily available in the United States, I found one almost immediately. I called Bruce Kintz to see if perchance there was one in their family library, and he told me that Sharon Robinson had brought one back from India with her. We contacted Sharon, who was then in Northern California, and she was very willing to lend me her copy. So, less than a week later, the book was in my hands.

Dr. Goel writes about his own kundalini arousal and describes his state at that time. (p. 27)

I am extremely restless.
I have a fear of death.
I cannot relax.
I have a fear of loneliness.
I have an extreme depression.
I am feeling extremely insecure.
I fear the environment around me.
I want immediate dependence and protection.

He also states that, even though he knew that he was into the kundalini process, and he was able to talk to some who had had encounters with others while they were experiencing the same process, he met with a lack of understanding all the same. On one occasion he spoke with a guru who should have recognized his condition, but that guru bluntly told him, "You do not appear to be one who is a deserving candidate for union with God. You go." Fortunately Goel took no offense. He explained away that guru's lack of understanding, saying, "The techniques of yoga are different. The grace of God for realizing Him comes in different ways, and it is always a secret between God and the one on whom the grace descends. Quite often the yogi understands his own experiences correctly and does not know exactly the experiences of others which are equally genuine and authentic and take the individual to God. Some of the yogis commit a great mistake when they try to generalize the total religious-spiritual knowledge on the basis of their own experiences and pass incorrect judgments about the experiences of others. They feel that what has not happened to them, perhaps does not exist, and cannot happen to anyone else." (p. 76)

Well, of course, Raye didn't have this problem. He was completely unaware of the kundalini process himself, had never thought of it in connection with his illness, and hadn't spoken to anyone else who might have had a clue that anything like this might be going on. I felt that if I mentioned it to the psychiatrists at the hospital that I would succeed only in making matters worse. The major benefit of this new idea was that my faith was strengthened, my surrender increased, and my ability grew to know that "All that is, is the work of God, and all is good."

Although nothing in the outer situation had changed, now I was able to relate many of the things which were going on to similar things that had happened to Dr. Goel. One of these was major. Day after day Raye accused me of infidelity. He was convinced that I was forming an alliance with his best friend, and he would describe our activities in great detail, even telling me the time when he saw his friend arrive at our house. He said that he could see everything clearly in his head and that it was useless for me to deny any of it. Occasionally he would become aware for a time that this was all a delusion. Then he would say, "It's all the mad, mad monkey mind," but when the hallucinations began again he would be totally convinced of their reality.

I recognized shortly after these illusions began that they paralleled his experience in his first marriage. Much to his distress, his wife had formed an alliance with his best friend, ultimately divorcing Raye and marrying the friend. Though he was separated from his children, whom he loved dearly, and he was left all alone, Raye had forgiven both his friend and his former wife, even graciously helping them to finally win the sanction of the Catholic church on their union. I'm sure that he thought he had completely released it all. However, it seemed evident that the pain had remained buried and that it must now be transcended. Dr. Goel helped me understand this through describing a similar experience of his own.

Then he explained:(p.220) "This long and painful happening brought to me the confirmation of a major fact which I had noticed again and again in the kundalini process. The Lord, out of His mercy, often creates external realities in accordance with the most deep-rooted mental formations of His chosen child by using individuals and materials in the external world so that the chosen child can relive and re-experience the past of this birth and previous births and can transcend it. [My own] case of infatuation was a similar case and was tailored, to my mind, for this purpose."

We might never know how many experiences of previous births were involved in this process, but it certainly seemed clear that this one involving marital infidelity was "tailored" to finally finish that particular illusion. There were others which I could not relate to anything in this life. For example, the fear that there were several men waiting outside with baseball bats and they were intent on beating him to death. The disinfectants at the hospital were poisons which "they" were putting in his room in order to kill him. For whatever reason, these fears had to be relived in order to be put aside forever.

Dr. Goel mentions frequently that the kundalini process involves continual ups and downs. This was true in Raye's experience. One of the beautiful things that happened during an "up" period was that Raye was able to tell a young man, who was in the hospital for a temporary problem, that there was an Avatar on the planet today. Of course, I don't know the details of this happening, but when I came to visit, the young man came up to me, his face beaming with joy, telling me that Raye had changed his whole life by telling him about Sathya Sai Baba.

As for me, I had gained faith and hope, but the situation itself remained unchanged. It was still important to me to hang on to all the Truth I knew. My many years in the study of Christian Science was very helpful. I remembered and re-read Mrs. Eddy's words:

> Job's faith and hope gained him the assurance that the so-called sufferings of the flesh are unreal. We shall learn how false are the pleasures and pains of material sense, and behold the truth of being, as expressed in his conviction, "Yet in my flesh shall I see God; that is, Now and here shall I behold God, divine Love....
>
> Suffering was the confirmation of Paul's faith. Through "a thorn in the flesh" he learned that spiritual grace was sufficient for him.
>
> Peter rejoiced that he was found worthy to suffer for Christ; because to suffer with him is to reign with him.

Sorrow is the harbinger of joy. Mortal throes of anguish forward the birth of immortal being; but God wipes away all tears.

The only conscious existence in the flesh is error of some sort--sin, pain, death--a false sense of life and happiness. Mortals, if at ease in so-called existence, are in their native element of error, and must become dis-eased, disquieted before error is annihilated.

--Mary Baker Eddy
Unity of Good, pp. 55, 57-58

The very circumstance which your suffering sense deems wrathful and afflictive, Love can make an angel entertained unawares.

--Mary Baker Eddy
Science and Health with Key to the Scriptures, p. 574

Arjuna, wear the armor of fortitude, and the blows of good and bad fortune can never harm you. Fortitude means equanimity in the face of opposites, putting up boldly with duality. It is the privilege of the strong, the treasure of the brave. The weak will be as agitated as peacock feathers; they are ever restless with no fixity even for a moment. They sway like the pendulum, this side and that, once toward joy, and the next moment toward grief.

Here some pause has to be made on one point. Fortitude is different from patience; fortitude is not the same as patience. Patience is putting up with something, tolerating it, bearing it, because you have no other choice. Having the capacity to overcome it, but yet disregarding it, that is the spiritual discipline, fortitude. Patiently putting up with the external world of duality, combined with inner equanimity and peace—that is the path to liberation. Bearing all—with analytic discrimination—that is the type of patience that will yield good results. Discrimination is the word used for this. It means the capacity to recognize what is called the nature of the objective world, that is to say, the world of objects that come and go and are not eternal. Generally, man seeks only happiness and joy; under no stress will he desire misery and grief. He treats happiness and joy as his closest well-wishers and misery and grief as his direst enemies. This is a great mistake. When one is happy, the risk of grief is great; fear of losing the happiness will haunt the man. Misery prompts inquiry, discrimination, self-examination, and fear of worse things that might happen. It awakens you from sloth and conceit. Happiness makes one forget one's obligations to oneself as a human being. It drags man into egoism and the sins that egoism leads one to commit. Grief renders man alert and watchful.

So, misery is a real friend; happiness spends out the stock of merit and arouses the base passions. So, it is really an enemy. Really, misery is an eye-opener; it promotes thought and the task of self-improvement. It also endows one with new and valuable experiences. Happiness draws a veil over experiences that harden a person and make him tough. So, troubles and travails are to be treated as friends, at least not as enemies. Only it is best to regard both happiness and misery as gifts of God. That is the easiest path for one's own liberation. Not to know this is basic ignorance. A person so ignorant is blind; actually, happiness and misery are like the blind man who must be accompanied ever by one who sees. When the blind man is welcomed, you have inevitably to welcome the man with eyes, for he is the constant companion of the blind man. So, too, happiness and misery are inseparable; you cannot choose only one. Moreover, misery highlights the value of happiness; you feel happy by contrast with misery." Thus said Krishna to Arjuna, to teach him the insignificance of duality.

--Sathya Sai Baba
Geetha Vahini, Chapter 4
American Translation by David Davidson

Chapter Six

PHYSIO-KUNDALINI SYMPTOMS

It was December, 1993, when the next breakthrough into understanding the physical phenomena came through another Baba devotee. This time through Dr. Dennis Gersten of San Diego. Dennis called to express his loving concern and to offer words of encouragement. Among other things, he told me that an excellent book on the kundalini had been written by Dr. Lee Sannella, entitled **The Kundalini Experience.** I ordered the book from the Bodhi Tree bookstore in Los Angeles and was able to begin reading it two days later.

From the first paragraph of the preface to the last paragraph of the tenth chapter, I was enthralled with what I was reading. In his first paragraph, Dr. Sannella likens the kundalini experience to human birth. He says that bleeding, moaning, crying, even screaming, accompany the birth of a new human being. Then should we be too surprised when muscle spasms, indescribable sensations, and sharp pains accompany a psychophysiological transformation, "a rebirth process as natural as physical birth.... Its initial stages often share the violence, helplessness, and imbalance that attend the start of extra-uterine human life."

I hadn't even finished the first page of the preface, but already I was relating to everything that was being said. When I had asked Swami "Does the illusion have to be so painful?" I was given His words, "...through loss of peace--even agony--an infant is born. The pains are worthwhile; they precede the birth of new life." If I could see all that was happening as a "birth of new life" rather than as an illness, could I not then enjoy it? I had spoken to Swami many times through my tears over the past months, saying, "Swami, I know that life is love, but I'm not enjoying it very much just now."

I've got to stop focusing on the pain and keep my attention on the gain. It had distressed me a lot to sit and watch the muscle spasms in Raye's chest, but now the doctor is telling me that muscle spasms are a symptom of transformation. He says, "It seems pathological only because the symptoms are not understood in relation to the outcome: a psychically transformed human being."

On page 29 of Dr. Sannella's book, I found the answer to the disturbing alternations of heat and cold in Raye's feet and legs. The doctor explains, "As the aroused kundalini current passes through each center (chakra), it temporarily energizes it and then, as it moves on, absorbs its energy. By the time the kundalini force reaches the topmost center, the rest of the body is depleted of bioenergy. The lower extremities tend to become cold and corpselike." In almost all of the case histories which Dr. Sannella recorded, intense heat was felt in some part of the body at some point in the process. Raye also complained of cramping. On page 46, Dr. Sannella states, "The life-force is hot, and it not only spreads its heat to different parts of the body, but it may even become bright and perceptible to the meditator.... When the life-force moves into obstructed areas, it induces painful and rather unpleasant sensations of roughness and cramping."

Referring to Gopi Krishna's recorded experience of the kundalini process, Dr. Sanella said that feelings of bliss were often "followed by feelings of terror, weakness, and indifference to people. His mouth tasted bitter, his throat felt scorched, and frequently his whole body felt as if it was pierced by countless hot pins. He suffered from insomnia. In the dark he noticed a reddish glow around himself. At times this was associated with severe back pains." (p. 51)

In a case history of a female in her late fifties, Dr. Sanella reports: "...she began to experience tingling in her arms and heat in her hands. Next she was unable to sleep for days, with energy surging through her whole body. She also had several dreams of having her consciousness separated from her body. A continuous loud sound started to appear inside her head. Soon there were cramps in her big toes, followed by vibratory sensations in her legs. Overnight, her big toes darkened, as if hit by a hammer, and eventually partially separated from the flesh." In Raye's case, all of his toenails darkened.

So, one by one, I found that every single symptom that my dear husband had been manifesting was part of what Dr. Sannella described as "an aspect of human psychospiritual unfolding that is intrinsically desirable." (p. 11) It was a powerful process of purification. Accepting that, I wondered what I might expect to happen next. Some people think that psychic powers result from kundalini arousal. However, Dr. Sannella says that the kundalini process is not necessarily connected with the appearance of psychic phenomena. (p. 10) Raye occasionally referred to feelings of bliss and to being bathed in golden light, but he did not report any dreamlike episodes.

I found the best answer to what the next stages of Raye's spiritual evolution might be in the words of another who has experienced the kundalini process. W. Thomas Wolfe stated: "The small self must dissolve--go away. And this is not something one can force or do. It is what remains when one just gives up and surrenders oneself to what will be. Slowly now, the light begins to dawn on me. My search winds down as the light of day begins to filter through the window." (p. 54)

And what will my role be in all of this? Of course, anyone who has studied Swami's teachings knows that the role of the observer is the ideal one. Abraham Maslow also knew the value of being the observer but he recognized the extreme difficulty we humans have in achieving this degree of detachment. Dr. Sannella says (p. 23) "Maslow held that the best possible avenue was to marshal our capacity for love in order to know and understand other human beings 'objectively.' He wrote: 'To the extent that it is possible to be non-intrusive, non-demanding, non-hoping...to that extent do we achieve this particular kind of objectivity.'"

In this case, to be "non-hoping" seems as unreachable a goal to me as enlightenment, but I resolve to make every effort.

* * * * * * * * *

The joy and pleasure earned by activities are only temporary. Nevertheless, one cannot desist from action, one should not desist from karma. How, then, is one to act? One should practice detachment and desirelessness towards the results of one's actions.

That is to say, one should treat all actions as yajnas, that is, performed for the glory of God and not for selfish ends; for earning lasting merit and not for temporary benefits. This type of action (nishkama karma) mentioned in the Gita is really the truest yajna. Action done in that spirit will not cause either greed or grief. It will cause only a sense of fulfillment of one's duty.

--Sathya Sai Baba
Sathya Sai Speaks, Vol. XI, Chap. 27, p. 158

Never slacken effort, whatever the obstacle, however long the journey. The goal will grow nearer faster than the pace with which you approach the goal. God is as eager to save you as you are eager to be saved; He is Love...

--Sathya Sai Baba
Sathya Sai Speaks, Vol. V, Chap. 43, p. 223.

GOLDEN LIGHT

Golden light, golden light,
Fill me with Your golden light.

Gentle eyes, gentle eyes,
Sathya Sai, such gentle eyes.

Holy feet, holy feet,
How I long to touch Your feet.

Be with me, be with me,
Lord of Lords, please be with me.

All my life, all my life,
Sathya Sai, You'll be my light.

Dennis Gersten

Chapter Seven

ACCEPTING THE GOAL OF LIBERATION

As my own anxiety decreased, I seemed to note a slight change in Raye also. Since I saw him only one hour per day, I could never be sure whether I was just witnessing an "up" moment or whether he was really improving. However, when during one visit he said, "I want you to go to India and talk to Baba for me," I felt that this was a definite sign of progress. He had previously expressed great fear that I would go to India and leave him behind. I was very cautious in regard to acting on this new request, however. The next day, he again repeated that he wanted me to go to India to talk to Baba. "What would you like me to tell Him or ask Him?" I inquired. "Just tell Him that I love Him and ask Him to give me liberation," he answered. When he continued to insist that he wanted me to go, I felt that it was necessary to speak to his doctor about it. I wasn't sure whether or not I might be needed for something in regard to Raye's care.

When I explained the situation to the hospital psychiatrist, he replied, "Mrs. Thomas, your husband is totally out of touch with reality at this time. We do not anticipate any possibility that he could be released in any less than two months, and, actually, we think that you might be looking at the need for long term care. If you feel that you should make this trip, this is the best time for you to go. We have made arrangements to transfer your husband to another hospital within the next few weeks, and he will be under treatment there for a minimum of two months."

Thus it was that I began to think about making arrangements to leave for India. All of our friends were uncomfortable with the idea of my going alone. Sharon Robinson had stayed with us and helped with Raye's care before his hospitalization, and she was willing to accompany me to India. The problem was that the tickets Raye and I had purchased, when we had thought that we would be spending Christmas with Swami, were non-refundable, non-exchangeable, and had almost reached their expiration date. I spoke with our travel agent. He was holding the tickets for us and was very willing to do anything he could to help us. However, he explained that it was impossible to change a name on a ticket (perhaps even illegal), and that in order to change my ticket and refund Raye's there would be heavy penalties.

Both Sharon and I felt that we could be sure of one thing: if Swami wanted us to come to India, He would open the way. Then Sharon said that she thought she would like to talk to someone at the airline about the situation. She put in the call, was connected with a very courteous, caring gentleman to whom she explained why it was impossible for Raye to use his ticket and why it was desirable for me to be accompanied on the long journey. The end result was that Sharon was assured that the airline would assist the travel agent in his efforts to make the tickets usable for our trip.

It was only a matter of hours before our travel agent called. He said, "Sai Baba must really want you to come to Him. In the history of my association with the airlines, I have never ever before known them to make it possible to change a name on a ticket. Both tickets will be reissued. They will no longer be non-refundable and non-exchangeable. They will be good for the period of time for which tickets are normally issued. Just let me know your leaving and returning dates, and I will send the tickets to you via overnight delivery." We had already made reservations to leave the following Monday, so we had no difficulty supplying the needed information.

The next day, January 11, when our dear friends Betty and Dave Davidson drove me to the hospital to see Raye, as they had been doing every day for almost two months, we expected that Raye would be happy to hear the news. But to our astonishment, when we arrived, we were the ones who were given news: "Your husband is being released today. Please wait while the doctor completes the instructions for his home care, and you may take him home with you." I wasn't sure how to react. Of course, if this meant that Raye had recovered, then I was overjoyed. However, the information that I was given didn't give me much encouragement. They said that Raye had decided that he wanted to leave, that they could not keep him against his wishes, and they were releasing him "against medical advice."

Raye was happy to be going home, but he still wanted me to go to India. It was clear, however, that he was not nearly ready to care for himself. He was extremely weak, could just barely walk, and was not able to pay attention to the details of personal grooming. We discussed several ways in which he might be cared for while I went on to India to talk to Swami, but he had reservations about all of them. He wanted to sleep most of the time. This, I knew, was a positive sign, because he had been unable to sleep for so long.

Neither Sharon nor I had the nerve to call the airline, so with only a few days left before we were scheduled to leave, we struggled to surrender it all to Swami, knowing that His will for all of us would be perfect. At this point, a whole band of angels stepped forward and pulled all of the pieces of this puzzle together. Mahri and Bruce Kintz said, "Since Baba's leelas opened the way for you and Sharon to travel to India, it would seem that you should go, and we feel strongly that it is Baba's will for Raye to stay with us while you're gone. It would be our pleasure to have him." Raye was delighted! He is never happier than when he is surrounded by children, and there are five in the Kintz family, ranging in age from five years old to nineteen. Each member of the family had participated in the decision, and they had unanimously voted to have Raye stay with them.

When Mahri had been preparing to visit Raye at the hospital one day, little Sean Timothy (Shanti), aged five, had asked what she was doing. Mahri had been getting some things together to take to Raye--some homemade cookies, a teddy bear with a picture of Swami on his chest, some candies and other goodies. So she told Sean she was going to take some things to Raye. Sean asked, "Why?" And Mahri replied, "To make him feel better." Sean went away. A few minutes later he came back to his mother, carrying his favorite toy--a large brown teddy bear. He handed it to Mahri saying, "If it will make Raye feel better, take him my teddy bear, too." This is the kind of family they are.

Jyoti, age ten, had taken all of her clothes and precious belongings out of her room, preparing to sleep on the living room sofa, so that Raye could have her room. This was done with a big happy smile. Ryan (Narayana) stood ready to do anything which he could do to help, including invite Raye to his eighth birthday party, which would take place while Raye was there. Josh and Tara were very much involved with their friends and activities, as young adults tend to be, but they made it clear that they were available to do anything possible for their house guest. Raye said that it was the only place he could have imagined staying.

So on Sunday, January 16, I drove Raye up the mountain to Idyllwild. He was still experiencing quite a bit of pain, still taking the anti-depressant medication prescribed by the doctor, still very tired and sometimes confused, but much more like himself than he had been for the past few months. If I had been going anywhere else in the world, other than to Swami's ashram, I could not have left him. Raye still wanted me to go, but he made me guarantee that I would be back in three weeks. That was the maximum time of separation he could imagine.

Our plane was scheduled to leave at 3:35 p.m. January 17. Sharon and I went to bed the night before, feeling that we had surmounted all of the hurdles and now all we had to do was lock the suitcases, ride to the airport, check in, and board the plane. We couldn't have been more wrong! At 4:30 a.m. we were jolted out of bed by a strong earthquake. After we decided there was no more sleep for us, we turned on the television to see if we could learn where the epicenter had been and whether or not there had been damage. Perhaps it had only been a strong aftershock from Big Bear or Yucca Valley, we thought. However, we soon learned that the epicenter had been in Northridge, that there had been extensive damage to freeways, and that the airport was closed! Again, we both surrendered the situation to Swami and waited with what we hoped was courageous patience.

Soon our friend Dave Davidson called. As he and his wife, Betty, were planning to drive us to the airport, he had been doing some checking. He said that the airport would be reopened in time for the flight and that he had worked out a route which would bypass the known freeway blockages. I, then, called the airline, and they assured me that the flight would be leaving on time. So, Sharon and I locked our suitcases, put them in the Davidsons' car, were driven safely to the airport, checked in, and boarded our flight to India.

Chapter Eight

LOVE IN ACTION

Our journey was pleasant and relatively uneventful. We arrived in Puttaparthi on the afternoon of January 20. The taxi stopped out in a field and motioned to some men standing by to take the wheelchair, me, and our luggage to the Accommodations Office. I felt a moment's nostalgia for the days when the taxi drove through the front gate and stopped in front of the Accommodations Office, where we picked up our key and continued on in the taxi to the Round House. But those days are gone forever, so gratitude for Sharon and the men who were helping us replaced my momentary regrets, and we started the trek to the office. The street was crowded, and it was obvious that there were numbers of people in the ashram, as there always are now, seeking the blessings of the Avatar.

Sharon disappeared into the Public Relations Office with our passports, and I sat outside watching the foot traffic. It seemed an awfully long time before she emerged from Public Relations and went into Accommodations. Again, there was what seemed to me to be an awfully long wait, but finally she came out smiling and holding up the key to our apartment for me to see. As she walked beside me on the way to the Round House, she related the adventures she had been having while I waited.

First, when she had entered the Public Relations Office, a large group was being processed. All of the usual little hitches were gradually overcome, the group work was finally complete, and then our passports were taken for the customary procedures. With the proper papers in hand, she had then gone on to the Accommodations Office. When she asked for the key to our apartment, the kind gentleman helping her had looked up to the board on which the key should be hanging and saw that it was not there. "Did Mrs. Thomas write to let us know that you and she were coming?" he asked. Sharon told him that our circumstances had been somewhat uncertain until the last moment before we left and that there just hadn't seemed to be time to let them know our intentions. He expressed compassion for our situation, but it would seem that the apartment must be occupied since the key was nowhere in sight. As he was talking, he opened a couple of drawers, looked in, closed them. Then, finally, without even looking down, he dropped his hand into a bucket at his feet which contained a large number of keys. He brought up one key, and glanced at it as if knowing already that it couldn't possibly be the one he was looking for, but it was! As much to his amazement as to Sharon's, within minutes all of the details were completed and we were on our way to the room.

We opened the door, sat the suitcases inside, turned around, and headed for darshan. We would just make it. Sharon was tired from the long trip, but she pushed the wheelchair down to the Poornachandra Auditorium, then up the slope to the shops, across to the spot by the ice cream store where the wheelchair ladies now wait to be admitted to darshan. After being searched, (a new experience for me as this procedure had only been initiated last summer after some youths, who Swami said had been motivated by jealousy, were able to enter the Mandir with knives) I was taken into the darshan area and placed in the back corner of the ladies area. When Swami came from the Poornachandra and entered what we used to call the "Ladies' Gate," he was at least a hundred feet away and kept his back to us as he spoke with the ladies who were seated immediately facing the front of the Mandir.

In previous years, there had been a section reserved for ladies who came in wheelchairs but who could sit on the ground. After darshan, I asked if it would be possible for me to sit on the ground. The answer was yes, but there didn't seem to be a specific location for this. I wondered how it would go and whether or not I would be able to deliver Raye's letter to Swami. Shortly before I had left, Raye had decided that it would be best for him to write directly to Swami himself, and so I had been entrusted with the precious letter.

The next morning my body didn't seem quite willing to sit on the ground, so I asked for a chair. I was given an excellent spot in the first arch, that is, to Swami's right as He enters the gate. It would not be possible to give Him the letter from there, but I would be able to see His face. To my great joy, He saw me. He flashed that incredible smile, and raised His hand in blessing. I sat there in bliss through darshan, after darshan while some very fortunate people were inside the interview room, through bhajans, and after bhajans until He returned to the Poornachandra. As I had hoped, He acknowledged my presence with a nod and a sweet smile. I left feeling that God was in the Poornachandra and all was right with the world, including Raye.

That afternoon I asked to sit on the ground. As the wheelchairs are brought in last, I was late and doubted that there would be a place for me where I might give Swami Raye's letter, but I was wrong. If Swami could guide the gentleman in Accommodations to the one needed key in a bucketful, could he not also find one needed seat for me in a packed darshan area? Through His instruments, the dear Seva Dals, He did. As He approached me, He reached out His hand and took Raye's letter very lovingly. I felt no doubt that He already knew every word it contained and that He was taking care, as He has so often told us He is.

However, when I arrived the next morning, the word was out that Raye was ill and that I had come to talk to Swami about it. The Seva Dals very lovingly guided me to a front seat immediately across from the veranda of the Mandir. When Swami came to where I was, He stood so close, His velvety divine feet were so inviting, that my planned speech was lost. Instead, I said, "Padnamaskar, Swami." He stood patiently while I held on to those precious Lotus Feet. When I came back to the world, I said, "Swami, husband very sick." He asked, "Where is he?" I replied, "California." Then, in the sweetest, most loving voice one has ever heard, He said, "Don't worry." He placed His hand on my head, patting it gently twice, then turned to go on down the line. After only a couple of steps, however, He turned back. With a quick motion of His hand, he manifested a large amount of snow white vibhuti, poured it all into my palm, and walked away. I knew instantly that He intended it for Raye, so I took a Kleenex from my purse, poured it from my palm to the Kleenex very carefully, and finally licked up the last few grains that remained on my hand.

When we returned to our room, Sharon found a small plastic vibhuti bag that still had a few grains of vibhuti remaining. We emptied that, shook it carefully, then poured the vibhuti from the Kleenex into the little bag. I placed it in my wallet, looking forward to the day when I could put it into Raye's hand.

Chapter Nine

"BEFORE THEY CALL, I WILL ANSWER"

The delight of being at Swami's ashram consists of a combination of little incidents, all of which give the opportunity to give love cr to receive love cr both. For example, one day when I was sitting on the ground, Swami threw candy for one of the devotees. Two pieces landed on my skirt, and I quickly put them away, thinking "One for Raye and one for me." When darshan was over, several ladies walked in front of me before I had gotten to my feet. Suddenly one of them reached into the folds of my skirt and brought out a piece of candy which I hadn't noticed. As she turned to walk away with it, I thought she looked a little guilty. So I spoke to her, saying, "Swami must have meant it for you, otherwise, I would have seen it." She smiled, and I had a wonderful sense of our oneness in God.

Shortly after Sharon and I had arrived, one of the ashram employees, Narasimalu, had come to help us in any way that he could. He pushed me in the wheelchair back and forth to darshan, bhajans, and the western canteen everyday, and on the few occasions when I had to go to the village, he took me there also. Sharon still pushed me to darshan in the morning, however, because we usually left the apartment before Narasimalu arrived. She began to experience some coughing and congestion several days into our stay, and one morning when she woke up she said, "Oh, dear, I just don't feel like getting out of bed this morning. I wouldn't even try, but you don't have any way to go to darshan." I tried to tell her not to worry that I'd figure out a way, but she was determined not to let me down. Just as she was forcing herself to get out of bed, someone knocked on the door. It was Narasimalu. He had been prompted to get up early that morning and had wanted to let me know he would be available to push me when I was ready to go to darshan. He continued to come early every morning then until our stay at the ashram came to an end.

Another day, we were without any bread in our apartment. It was our custom to have breakfast and lunch in the western canteen, but usually our dinner consisted of a vegetable or coconut roll from the ashram bakery. It wasn't at all unusual to have to stand in line for fifteen minutes or so before being waited on at the bakery, and Sharon still didn't feel quite up to doing that. As we were wondering how we might get some bread, we agreed that what we really needed was someone with strong, young legs, who was willing to stand in line.

That afternoon, when we answered a knock on our door, a young lady had come "to meet the author of the books." We welcomed her. She told us that her name was Irini, that she had immigrated from Poland to Australia, that she loved reading books about Swami, and that she loved talking and hearing about Baba. So, the three of us had a wonderful time sharing Baba stories. As she was leaving, she turned and asked, "Is there anything you need? I'd be happy to do some shopping or run some errands for you." Sharon and I looked knowingly at each other as we gave our biggest, happiest smiles to our visitor. When we asked if she could pick up a few items for us from the bakery, she said, "Of course! I go to the bakery every day, so it will be no trouble at all. Just let me know what you want, and I'll bring it after bhajans." And so she did, and continued to bring us fresh bread every day until she returned to Australia.

On one morning when I was sitting on the ground in darshan, Swami came close and I asked Him, "Swami, will you see us?" He replied promptly and emphatically, "Yes, I will see you." He gave me that entrancing, divine smile, tapped me lightly on the top of my head, and walked on down the line to bring joy to the others who were waiting. Looking back, I can see that my question showed my lack of understanding. I asked, "Will you see us?" when He was seeing us many times a day. Whatever we asked, He granted. Whatever name or form we saw, it was He.

A dear lady from Great Britain invited me to join their group for a tour of Swami's spectacular new hospital. Even though, I'm sure that I caused them a lot of extra work, they made me feel so welcome. The hospital is a constant source of joy and wonder, and our visit was a true blessing.

Then the postman knocked on our door and handed me an envelope. What a delight that he delivered it! Had it been held for pickup, which is the way much of the mail in the ashram is handled, I wouldn't even have thought to look for it. It was a birthday card from Raye which had come from Idyllwild, California, USA to Puttaparthi, Andhra Pradesh, India in eight days! Raye told me that he was happy, that he was feeling much better, and that he loved me. What else could I possibly ask for? The wonderful words of the Ninety-First Psalm came back to me, and I felt that Swami was speaking to me about Raye, "Because he hath set his love upon me, therefore will I deliver him; I will set him on high because he hath known my name. He shall call upon me, and I will answer him; I will be with him in trouble; I will deliver him and honor him. With long life will I satisfy him and show him my salvation." (Holy Bible, Psalms 91:14-16) In afternoon darshan, Swami gave me a smile which seemed to say, "You see? I told you not to worry."

The next day I was happy and relieved about Raye, but I still had a strong desire to talk to Swami about everything that had happened. When He came near, I said, "Many questions, Swami." He asked, "When are you leaving?" I replied, "In a week." He responded, "Ah, one week." Then He manifested vibuthi which He gave me and several others. That made it clear that the vibhuti was for me this time and not a special formula for Raye, so I quickly ate it all. What a generous, magnanimous Lord is our Lord!

On February 3, I was allowed to sit in the front row with my birthday candy. The Seva Dals assured me that it didn't matter that it was one day early. This way I would have the blessed candy all day on the anniversary of my birth. And so it was that when Swami came, he threw my birthday candy, blessed my medallion, took some letters, and then asked, "When are you going back?" I told Him that I would be there two more days. This time He conveyed the message to me somehow that it was time for me to go home to Raye, but I still prayed to speak to Him at greater length.

On my birthday, just at lights out (9:00 p.m.), our neighbor across the atrium came to our door, calling my name on the way. He said, "Come quickly. There's a call for you from the States." I ran! It was Raye. He had called to tell me how much he wished for me to have a very happy birthday, and he wanted to assure me that he was recuperating very rapidly. He told me what a wonderful time he was having at the Kintzes, but went on to say that he was looking forward to my being home. I also spoke to Mahri, and she confirmed that Raye was happy and healthy. It was the best birthday present I could ever have been given.

The day after my birthday, Sharon and I were contemplating our dinner of vegetable rolls, and Sharon said, "You know, as delicious as they are, I don't think I can face a roll for dinner tonight. I would love to have a real meal. Almost on cue, we heard a knocking on our door. It was our dear neighbors who had called me into their home to receive a call on their telephone the night before. They said that, knowing I had just had a birthday, they wanted to present us with a birthday meal, howbeit a day late. And what a wonderful meal it was. The food was nourishing, prepared and presented with love, but that was not all. Again, I remembered words that I had memorized in my Bible classes so many years ago: "And I will rejoice in Jerusalem, and joy in my people; and the voice of weeping shall be no more heard in her, nor the voice of crying....And it shall come to pass that, before they call, I will answer; and while they are yet speaking, I will hear." (Holy Bible, Isaiah 65:19,24.)

On many days I had sat next to Jyothi Rajagopal in darshan. She was aware that I had come to speak to Swami about my dear sick husband. Being without her own beloved husband, as well as being a lady characterized by love and compassion, she watched every day for any sign that Swami might call me for interview. On the morning before I was to leave, Swami had called several people for interview. While they waited on the veranda, he walked over, looked toward the ladies near the gate, and signaled for one to come. We all looked to see who he was calling, but no one got up. Jyothi touched me on the arm and said, "Go, He's calling you!" I whispered, "I wish you were right, but I don't think so." He signaled again. This time the head Seva Dal, went to the veranda to see who he wanted. She came back and looked around, but did not find the person she sought. Jyothi got up from her seat, went to the nearest Seva Dal, and said, pointing to me, "There she is. That's the one Swami wants." The Seva Dal told her, "I don't think so. He said that she was an Indian woman from America." Jyothi came to me asking, "Do you have any Indian blood?" I thought she was joking, so I answered, "Well, there may be a little American Indian blood somewhere in my ancestry." "That's good enough, go!" she replied emphatically.

Such an adorable lady! Such love she obviously felt for Swami. And such compassion for His devotees who always want more and more of His time and attention. It wasn't me that He was looking for, but in the name and form of Jyothi Rajagopal, He gave me as much love as if He had called me in. I have never before been able to be so happy when <u>not</u> called for interview.

And I have never before experienced so completely that all names and forms are His.

As I pondered the incredible love that was being expressed toward Raye and me, the sense of there being many people involved in this generous outpouring of compassion was uppermost in my thought. In India and Croatia, in Argentina and Germany, in Italy and Great Britain, in Australia and The Netherlands, in Canada and New Zealand, in Hong Kong and Japan--devotees of Sathya Sai Baba had been praying for us.

Individuals who had done so much for us in a practical way stood out in my memory. I saw each in his human form and called each by name. But, as my gratitude for these beautiful souls increased, my consciousness of their separateness decreased. Little by little, all forms merged into One and I knew that One to be Love. This sense of Oneness brought about great bliss. As I so often do, afterward I tried to capture it in words. My efforts are pale and grossly inadequate in comparison with the glory of the experience, but I record them on the following page in the hope that they may provide a glimpse into what was, for me, a milestone in my journey Spiritward.

The Form He Takes

Whether we wake or lie asleep
In bliss so high or pain so deep,
He is here; He's always near.
Love's His form.

Whether we're close or far apart
In sorrowful mind or blissful heart,
He is there, and He does care.
Love's His form.

Whatever the name, the caste, the race,
When compassion glows from any face,
He does abide deep inside.
Love's His form.

Chapter Ten

BABA'S CONSTANT CARE
by
Mahri Kintz

Our family had known Raye for ten years before these unusual happenings took place. We loved him very much. Raye had always been such a giver. Now that he was in need, how could we give to him? We watched him as he was going through this major transformation, and we felt so helpless. We couldn't even think of any way to alleviate Joy's distress. We could only surrender our will to Baba's and trust His mysterious leela. We prayed and assisted in small ways like cleaning house or bringing food. As we are all one, anyone's growth or difficulties affect us. All of the members of the Cherry Valley Sai Baba Center, of which Bruce was the president, were involved. After all, the Thomas home was our meeting place. We were all growing and changing during this experience.

On New Year's Eve I went to bed after offering a fervent prayer for Raye and the whole world. I also asked Baba to give me a New Year's resolution. He came in a dream. We were in a ballroom, and everyone was dancing. Raye and I were sitting at the side like wallflowers. Suddenly I saw Baba. He was seated in a chair in the center of the dance floor. I said, "Raye, there's Baba!" and we walked over. I pleaded with Swami, "Baba, will you help Raye?" He looked at Raye so lovingly. Then, looking deeply into my eyes, He said, "I am always taking care."

My sister appeared at our side, and I realized that the only ones I recognized in this dream were my family. Suzanne asked, "Baba, what should I do?" Looking at both of us, He chanted slowly, "Sooooo Hummmmmmm." At that moment, our clock must have struck midnight. I could hear the New Year's party in a nearby gym, noise-makers, horns honking, and people singing "Auld Lang Syne." I woke up very happy. Not only did I get the reassurance that Baba was taking care of Raye, but I was given my New Year's resolution also--to chant the So Hum mantra daily.

I hesitated to tell Joy the dream because I couldn't understand why I received the consolation from Baba and why she didn't even appear in the dream. Baba's reasons later became quite clear. As a speaker at our Center recently said, "Swami is not only omnipresent and omnipotent, He's also omni-competent!"

When I arrived at the Center January 11 (Bruce was out of town), I was shocked to see that Raye was at home. Was he well enough to be out of the hospital? What would this do to Sharon and Joy's trip? Even as I asked the questions, I was witnessing Joy's reaction to these sudden developments: the degree of her equanimity was, to me, a clear example of what Baba expects from His devotees. Joy attended to Raye as the Center members arrived. When she came in for study circle, she looked at me with her eyes wide, her shoulders raised, as if to say, "I surrender. What else can I do?" Whether she would leave for India in less than a week, as had been planned, or stay home to care for her husband, she was content for Sai's will to be done.

As I closed my eyes to meditate, I felt Baba asking me to take care of Raye. It seems that if I want Baba to say "Yes" to me, then I need to say "Yes" to Him. I have complete confidence that, if Baba gives us an assignment, it won't be more than we can handle. He will give us the extra strength and ability to meet the challenge. A few details had to be addressed, however. I am not one alone; I'm part of a unit: our family. Each member has to be working harmoniously for the task to be successful. So, the next day, after discussion and voting, we were all united in one final vision: Swami's will.

There was still one more obstacle to the plan, however, in that my parents were scheduled to arrive on Saturday from the Midwest for their annual visit to the grandchildren. I couldn't quite see how all this could work out. Raye would need to be nestled down comfortably at home, but my parents would undoubtedly want to be going places and doing things. When I called my mother to discuss it with her, before I could lay out the problem, she said, "Oh, we've changed our minds about coming." What a solution to my dilemma! This was just another sign that proved to me that Swami was taking care and that He wanted me to be His instrument in this instance.

Joy brought Raye to us here in the mountains. I call it Prasanthi Idyllwild. There is fresh air, mountain spring water, and nature all around. What a place for healing. Baba had planned it all so beautifully. Joy had a renewed exuberance. With the expectation of seeing our Lord and gratitude for her husband's improved health, she had so much more energy. She was now doing many of the things which Raye had always done for her, and I felt that Baba had given her a new freedom. Raye very softly asked me, "How do you feel about my being here?" He was in such a state of selflessness. I felt that Baba had given us a precious treasure to care for. We were all very happy.

On Joy's departure day, Los Angeles was struck by what is now called the Northridge earthquake, and there were lots of intense vibrations all around. Bruce was working out of town, and by nighttime, I was restless. I could sense the tumult from the quake victims, and some kind of fear came over me. I began to pray for them. I knew that Sai was looking after them, but still I felt tremendous concern for the many devotees in the area. I was also feeling nervous about Raye. "What if he wandered away and got lost or got sick again?" I thought. Then, as I prayed, Swami's words from the dream swept over me like a calming, warm blanket: "I am always taking care." How comforting is our Mother Sai. She will take care of all of us. Faith in Baba brings so much peace. One Sai brother, whose home had been affected by the quake, told us later that the shattered mirror that fell on him felt like rose petals.

Raye's stay with our family is a story of love and joy. Even though he was still a little weak and unsteady, a little forgetful about things like closing the refrigerator door and turning off the water, caring for him was no more difficult than keeping an eye on the children. I observed him to be so egoless, so much in the heart. He just sort of melted and blended into the family. At times he was almost invisible. On one morning, when the bathroom was occupied for quite a while, he became completely invisible. He had disappeared entirely. My heart skipped a beat. I sent one of the children out to search for him. As we are surrounded by forest, it's easy to get lost. I called Raye's name, and he appeared in the yard, smiling so sweetly and humbly. "I had to go find a bush," he responded to my worried look. How flowing and adaptable he was. How harmonious and peaceful the world would be if all the individuals in it could be flexible and put the needs of others before their own, as Raye was constantly doing.

One evening at dinner, the boys were telling Raye how much fun it was to have him here. They asked, " Raye, would you be our dad while Daddy's gone?" Raye's face lit up. He just beamed, and his whole aura puffed up with pink. He answered, "Why, sure." What a healer love is! The children were letting Raye know that they loved and needed him, and Raye was letting them know that he loved them, too.

Even though we took morning walks while Sean T. rode his bike, and Raye helped me with the cooking, I knew that he needed something more to do with his time. Baba has said that in this world we need to act. He has also said that if we can't quiet the mind, do some work. Raye had a lot of time on his hands, and I was kept very busy. I would give him little things to do such as sweeping or folding laundry, but what would he like to do? Then the inspiration came: the video camera! We went to his house to get it, and what fun! Now he could go outside, film the children playing, the trees, the snow. He did a wonderful job of capturing Narayana's eighth birthday party. He was participating and appreciating everything through the lens of his camera, and he was truly enjoying himself.

Oh, yes, there was snow. A storm came and dumped eight inches or so. Raye watched it come down and cover the landscape, calling it "the million dollar view." When the phone rang, Raye answered, "Is this angel number four?" It was my sister, Suzanne. When she paused before answering the question, Raye's quick comeback was, "Well, at least you're in the top ten." Suzanne lives a few minutes away in a little cabin across the lane. She is an artist, and she makes beautiful native American Indian pine needle baskets, collecting the needles from local pine trees. She had called to invite Raye to come make a basket. How Baba thinks of everything! This would not only be a wonderful meditative time for them, but it would also allow me to get some things done around the house. I know other mothers and homemakers feel as I do that it's hard to elevate our somewhat menial tasks of cleaning and washing to the level of worship, but I do work at treating this job as a high calling from the Lord. Baba has said, "Wife is the illumination of the home," and, if I think and act as if He is coming to dinner, then I can cook and clean and serve all the little Babas with deep reverence and joy. I like to vacuum with bhajans blaring, so this gave me a chance to do my homemaker's dance without disturbing Raye.

For a full week, Raye would don Josh's snowboots and his coat and walk up to Suzie's and quietly work with his hands in accordance with my sister's instructions. I wish you could have seen his face and his happy sense of accomplishment, as well as Joy's face when she received the basket from him as a birthday present when she returned from her trip to see Baba. She said that although Raye has given her many things in their years together, this was the first gift she had received that he had made with his own hands. She values it now among her most prized possessions. The joy of Joy!

To watch Raye's continued improvement made me so happy. Even though we were all making little sacrifices to have him with us, they were more than balanced by the reward we were feeling in our hearts. No wonder Baba says sacrifice can bring happiness. Since Joy was at the Lotus Feet, we were feeling Baba strongly. We would daily talk about what they were doing. "They're in darshan now," we'd say as we pondered the Presence. We'd watch movies of Baba and talk about Him. Bruce had finished his out-of-town job, and he had a special friendship with Raye. They would go places together. Raye found pleasure even in a trip to the hardware store.

Raye was so very much in the present moment. I would observe him as he would interact with everyone, sort of like Baba does. You know how sometimes you feel one-on-one with Baba, like He's deeply interested in you, really present with you? In this world, we so often forget to "be here now." Raye didn't forget. He would be with Tara, who was a high school senior, discussing her studies, her college or career plans. He was genuinely interested. He talked to Josh and Bruce about their work. He participated in the children's activities and was always there for them. He was involved in the family without any sense of attachment.

There were periods when Raye would seem temporarily far away or pensive. He is not a talker, so you cannot really tell what's going on in his mind. One day in particular, during his last week with us, he went into a slump. I felt concerned, but I tried to stay detached. The lesson to not get involved in other people's dramas is a tough one for me. Shirdi Baba used to say, "Let the world go topsy turvy, you stay where you are." The way I manage this is to get some distance (from the mind, probably), send light, and pray. I felt intuitively that Raye was missing Joy. I prayed intensely to Baba for help, some news or something! All day I concentrated on this. In the evening we received a call from Vidya Alekal, who had just returned from India. "I have a message from Joy," she related. Raye perked up immediately. Vidya said, "Joy said to tell you that she loves you." And she went on to tell us that Baba had spoken to Joy in darshan and said, "I will see you." Oh, thank you, Baba. Raye was so cheered up that he could hardly sleep that night. Little did Vidya know that she had been such an instrument of His Love.

On February 4, Raye called Joy in India, and they both enjoyed the talk so much. The next day, a letter which Joy had written on the plane and mailed in Kuala Lumpur on January 19 arrived. It had taken eighteen days for it to get here, but it was certainly welcomed when it finally came.

The day before Joy returned, the First Sunday Sai Baba Meeting was held at the Ebell Club. Rita and Robert Bruce were the speakers, and the Cherry Valley Center was hosting the meeting. Raye was a shining light, a new man, a walking miracle! Dressed in his white shirt and orange Seva Dal scarf, he was ushering and greeting devotees with a big smile. He told Shakuntala Patel, "Yup, they gave me a job. I get to do seva." I guess Baba is working with all of us, clearing away the accumulated debris of our illusions, so that we can do His seva. The next day when Raye returned to his home and his Joy, I could truly say, "Family life is work, but it's worth it!" I know that doing everything for God is the way to live. It can transform our lives into pure heaven if we will just let it be so. Life is Love, and we are definitely enjoying it. Thank you, Baba.

* * * * * * * * *

When one's inner reactions and agitations are transmuted into Divine, all that one experiences through the senses, the mind, and the intellect, take on the Divine luster, reveal their Divine core, and man is shaped in the mold of Love. One can be in the world and yet be unaffected by it, provided this vision is gained. All activity will then be for the Almighty, by His grace, and through His will. Do not get work done through cooks, servants, ayahs, and others, in the home; women must not depend on these, for the care of their children or attendance on their husbands. Earning leisure for meditation through these servants is not a spiritual gain. Do all the household work as acts of worship for Him; that is more fruitful than hours of meditation, hours gained by entrusting this precious work to paid helpers. Men, too, must feel that frittering away precious time, flitting from one vanity to another and seeking more and more purposeless means of spending days and nights is detrimental to the main aim of life. Spread joy, give strength, distribute courage, console the distressed, help the lame to walk and the blind to see—that is the real timetable of the activities of man.

--Sathya Sai Baba
Sathya Sai Speaks, Vol VII, Chap. 28, pp. 146

Chapter Eleven

TO HIS LOTUS FEET

Raye's own estimate of his three weeks with the Kintz family was that it was a mountaintop experience in more ways than one. The topic of conversation was Baba, the forms were Baba, and Love was always and everywhere in evidence. There is no doubt that his being with the family was an integral part of the Sai Mother's plan for his healing.

Another evidence of this took place in the experience of another Center member, Mercedies Swift. Mercedies has a background in astrology, and she had been telling us for several weeks that every ten years certain key stars and planets come into perfect alignment, creating an unusually strong divine energy. While it lasts for a period of only twenty-four hours, in that time spiritual aspirants have an opportunity to utilize this energy to deepen their meditation and to draw closer to the Sai Mother in Love and Wisdom.

As the Center members had all been engaging in prayer for Raye's healing, Mercedies did not want to allow this opportunity to pass without utilizing it for Raye's benefit. She began to intensify her prayerful meditations seventy-two hours before the stars and planets were to come into the rare alignment. On the morning of the awaited day, as she was pondering Baba's power and love in relation to Raye, she felt a strong message in her heart. She told me, "Raye's healing will be rapidly realized only in a family setting." At the time, it meant very little to me, as there is no "family setting" which would be available to either Raye or me among our relatives. However, in retrospect, since the day of the astral alignment was January 11, Mercedies meditation took place in the morning and Raye was suddenly and unexpectedly released from the hospital the same afternoon, it would certainly seem that he was destined to go into the family setting for the rapid realization of his perfection. As Alfred, Lord Tennyson, said, "More things are wrought by prayer than this world dreams of."

There is no doubt in my mind but that Baba heard and answered every prayer, including my own. When I went to darshan just before leaving the ashram, I took several things that I had brought for Baba to bless. He sweetly placed His hand on them in a generous blessing, but He walked away without any further words.

I was reminded of the experience I had on an earlier occasion when I had been so intent on giving Him a letter. The letter explained how important it was for Him to take certain steps so that the Sathya Sai Book Center of America would have permission to distribute one of the books I had written. He ignored me completely when He passed in darshan that morning, and I was sure that He meant not to grant the boon I craved. However, only a few minutes after darshan, I was given the news that everything I had asked for in the letter had been done. It is clear that we will never understand why He does certain things the way He does, and it is useless to try. All we can do is just love His uncertainty.

Devotee David Davidson has had similar interaction with Swami. Prior to his first visit to Baba,

Dave was diagnosed with lymphoma (a type of cancer). He had been treated with chemotherapy and told that the cancer was in complete remission. When he went to India in 1988, he was hospitalized with gastro-enteritis and hepatitis, which was pronounced cured before he returned to the States. However, shortly after his return, a very annoying rash appeared on his face. Various topical treatments were administered by a dermatologist but no improvement was forthcoming.

In 1991, in an interview, Baba placed His hand on Dave's head, held his hand, and spoke the reassuring words, "I am helping. I am taking care." However, the skin eruptions continued. In the following two years, specialists were consulted and ten biopsies were performed. The first nine were negative; the last was positive. Thus, the oncologist told Dave that the condition was lymphoma. A board of dermatologists agreed that the diagnosis was cancer and that everything that could be done was being done. In effect, they held out little hope of improvement or cure.

Therefore, when Dave went to visit Baba in 1993, he prepared three letters. In one, he asked Baba to heal the cancer. In the second, he said, "Since You have not taken the letter in which I requested healing of cancer, may I assume that I will not be healed?" And the third letter was a letter expressing gratitude for whatever Baba's decision might be. He took the first letter to darshan a number of days. Even though Baba might easily have taken it on several different occasions, He did not. Finally Dave brought the second letter, offered it, and Swami took it immediately. The third letter, which was really a letter of surrender, was also accepted promptly. Dave assumed that Baba had declined to heal his cancer, and he accepted the decision with reasonable equanimity.

A year later, while Dave was visiting his daughter in a city in Northern California, his son-in-law questioned the diagnosis of cancer. The skin problem was still very much in evidence, and Dave's daughter said that they had a dermatologist they respected very highly and she couldn't understand why it had never occurred to her to mention him to her Dad previously. With encouragement from his family, Dave made an appointment to see his daughter's dermatologist. The doctor examined the condition, examined records of the extensive blood tests which had been done, and concluded that there was no cancer. He said that he agreed with the statement which had been made by the Davidsons' family doctor, "Anyone with that blood chemistry could not have lymphoma." He prescribed a topical treatment. Of the dozen or more of such creams which had been applied before, nothing had helped at all. However, following the application of this cream, the condition which had persisted for five years, cleared up within a few days.

Did Baba refuse to take the letter which asked him to heal cancer because there was no cancer to heal? Or did he refuse to take the letter because he had already healed the cancer? Or could it have been because He does not give repeated assurances (as Dr. Goel mentioned in **Third Eye and Kundalini,** p. 89)? We may never know. The only thing that we can really be sure of is this: When Baba says, "I am taking care," you can be sure that everything that happens afterward will somehow be for your greatest good--no matter how it may appear at the moment.

During the months of Raye's illness, many dire predictions were made--both for his physical and mental health. Painkillers and anti-depressant drugs were prescribed for his continuous use. Today, however, he uses simple exercises for his back and legs, chants the Gayatri, repeats the name, and does pranayama, alternate nostril breathing. He takes no medication.

One of the books which was recommended to us was **The Way Home** by Gloria St. John, a Baba devotee in Northern California. Gloria recommends alternate nostril breathing for balancing the chakras. She says, "Alternate nostril breathing stimulates the flow of ida and pingala [energy impulses running parallel to the spine] and, in so doing, shifts our energy to the ajna center [the sixth chakra]. To do it, sit comfortably and block the right nostril with your thumb. Inhale through the left, exhale, and inhale again. Hold the breath and block the left with your finger. Exhale through the right, inhale, block. Exhale left, inhale, block. Complete ten sets and feel the energy flow." (p. 118)

When I read that, I remembered an incident which had occurred in one of our interviews with Baba. A lady had told Him that she experienced a constant clicking in her head (a kundalini phenomenon mentioned by Dr. Sannella). Baba told her to do alternate nostril breathing and demonstrated it, to the best of my memory, just as described above.

* * * * * * * * * *

> Curled at the base of the spine are the opposing energy impulses called ida and pingala. One is positive,

or male, the other negative, or female. They wind around the sushumna, the central energy column in the etheric, parallel to the spine. In the normal course of life, breath moves prana or life energy up and down this column quite safely. Spiritual practice accelerates our ability to access prana so the energy columns become more active. This is highly beneficial because the greater activity breaks down the etheric webs of energy which separate the chakras from each other and keep us stuck at the lower levels of consciousness.

--Gloria St. John
The Way Home, p. 116

The spinal column of man, ending with the "thousand-petaled lotus" [seventh chakra] in the brain is very much like a serpent poised on its tail with the hood widely spread. In the science of Kundalini Yoga, the vital energy of man, lying dormant like a coiled snake at the bottom of this column in the first chakra, is awakened and aroused so that it courses up through six more chakras (centers of superior consciousness) until it reaches the "thousand-petaled lotus" chakra at the very top of the skull. The passage for the kundalini is through the sushumna nerve in the center of the spinal column.

--Sathya Sai Baba
Sathya Sai Speaks, Vol. IX, Chap. 6, p. 37

Chapter Twelve

EXPANSION LOVE

Coming home to find Raye back to his normal self again was an extremely happy experience. From our first day at home in Cherry Valley together, all of the things which had been taken away during the previous year began being restored very quickly. One of those things was Raye's driver's license. When it had come up for renewal on September 25, 1993, he had been neither physically nor mentally able to cope with the required test. Now that he was feeling perfectly fit, he took the test, passed it with no difficulty, and became a licensed driver again.

He had also lost the opportunity to travel to India to see his beloved Swami in the fall of 1993, and he was eager to have that loss restored. He promptly began exploring various travel arrangements. Though he was now in perfect health, his energy was still somewhat depleted from the long months of illness. Therefore, he decided that we should travel with a group so that there would be others available to help should we not be able to manage everything ourselves.

However, the greatest transformation which had occurred over the past year was Raye's complete change of attitude about the length of our stay in India. Whereas, previously he had been quite content to be with Swami six weeks or so, now he was inquiring how long the airline tickets would be valid. Finding the length of time to be four months, he made our return reservations on the last possible day before the tickets would expire. Not only was he willing to go for the maximum period of time, but he repeatedly said that if Swami would allow him the opportunity to serve (that is, give him a specific job to do) that he wanted to stay in India permanently. Prior to this time, he had not been willing to even discuss the possibility of a lengthy stay--much less a change of residence. It was obvious that some deep inner changes had taken place during the past year.

Interestingly, expanded love occurred not only in Raye's experience, but also in the experience of others who had played a role in his transformative process. It had been our friend Crystal Pearl who had been with us when Raye overdosed for the second time. Knowing that the process included mandatory hospitalization and how much Raye despised being hospitalized, I had hesitated to call for emergency help again. However, Crystal felt that she was obligated to call 911 for assistance, and so she did.

Later, she and her husband Brian traveled in the same group that Raye and I had chosen to join. Since her story is unique and very personal, I asked her if she would write it and allow me to include it in this book. In her great gratitude to Swami for this step in her own transformative process, she kindly consented to do so. The next chapter is her story.

* * * * * * * * *

> "I will restore to you the years that the locust hath eaten...."

The Holy Bible, Joel 2:25

Chapter Thirteen

9-1-1

by

Crystal Pearl

As the plane was landing in Bangalore, the flight number, 911, was circling my mind. On this flight was a group of thirty devotees from Southern California. Included in the group were Joy and Raye. What I did not know then was that this was to be the very best of the five trips I have taken to see Sai Baba. What I did know was that the numbers 9-1-1 evoked a painful memory of the day in Cherry Valley when I called emergency services because Raye appeared to have attempted suicide.

My experience with the field of mental health is probably greater than most lay people's due both to personal experiences with bipolar disorder (a form of depression) and to two years' experience of volunteering on the local suicide crisis hotline. As a telephone volunteer, I needed to call the police by dialing 911 on several occasions. Although it was never routine, when I made that call for my friend Raye, it seemed to be the most difficult task that I ever had to do.

When I was younger, I had suffered through many hospitalizations due to bipolar disorder. My parents, often against my will, had the authorities keep me in the hospital for long periods of time, so I well know how difficult that can be. Yet, Raye had obviously lost control and his wife and his many friends were terribly concerned that he refused to voluntarily admit himself for treatment.

I had come to their home that day with the intention, and with Joy's permission, to try to get him to place himself in a private hospital. I had placed a call to the hospital and was waiting for the doctor to notify us that a bed was available. The wait seemed endless. Raye was definitely not himself. He spoke of dying and reincarnating. A friend had brought lunch and, after eating, remained to talk with us. Raye left the room for a short time. When he returned, he kissed Joy goodbye and lay down in front of the altar.

At first, we thought he was going to take a nap. Then it became clear that he had taken something. Joy discovered that there were several over-the-counter sleep medications missing. Raye told us that he had taken them. I called poison information and they said that such a dose might not cause any harm but that he should go to emergency anyway to get checked out. Raye refused to go.

Then the friend followed Raye to another room and returned with a handful of what looked like prescription pills in her hand. She had taken them from Raye. They were all sorts of sizes and colors. Now I was quite concerned as to exactly what Raye had taken. He could possibly have taken a lethal dose. I told everyone that I was going to call 911 for emergency assistance. Everyone asked me not to do this, but I felt that, given the circumstances, I had no choice but to try to preserve Raye's life. I dialed 911.

When the paramedics arrived, Raye lay calmly on the couch answering their questions. He was not at all clear in his mind. When asked who the president of the United States was, he answered that it was Ronald Reagan instead of Bill Clinton. Joy was extremely upset, as it seemed that Raye would be taken back to the mental health center.

Dave Davidson arrived and he, too, was concerned. He said to me, "I wish you hadn't done that." I felt that I had become the bad guy and that everyone I knew would hate me for the rest of my life. Yet, I was very aware inside that Swami had sent me there that day. I could never have imagined that it would turn out this way.

After the ambulance took Raye, Joy requested to be alone. I drove home. I felt terrible. At the same time, something was lifting from my shoulders. It was a strange, almost indescribable feeling. I realized that I had just done to someone I loved the same thing that my parents had done to me. Suddenly I felt a rush of love toward my parents such as I had never felt before. The deeply buried, potent anger that had prevented me from fully loving them all these years, had left me.

When I reached home, I called my mother. I tried, unsuccessfully, to explain to her what had happened. Finally I realized that her understanding what had happened was not important. The important thing was that I now understood that they had hospitalized me only because they were concerned for my welfare. I realized how difficult that must have been for them. Now, because of calling 911 for Raye, my love for my elderly parents has expanded.

My relationship with them now is better than it has ever been. I could never have planned for anything like this to happen. It can only be the Grace of Sai.

* * * * * * * * *

...Seva opens the eyes of man to the comprehensive unity of creation.... The Vedas declare that the mother and the father have to be revered as Divine and foster the blooming of that Divine Principle.... The duty that each one owes to himself is to clear the heart of fear and grief and to fill it with Love and Dedication.... The easiest and most fruitful expression of Dharma today consists in Seva, service as worship of the Divine around you. Dedicate all your skill, talents, wealth, and scholarship to the living embodiments of Divinity that are around you. That is the Dharmashakti (power of right activity) which can draw Grace upon you.

The Universe is seen; it can be learned about; it can be experienced and enjoyed. But God is unseen. He has to be inferred through His handiwork. So, too, society to which social service is rendered cannot be seen as such. We can contact only individuals. But, through the individual, you infer the immanence of the Divine. All are actors on the world stage, in His play. Every atom is surcharged with His Power, His Might, His Glory. Every being is surcharged with His Bliss, His Beauty, His Goodness. Do not claim that you are using some skill or force which is especially yours; it has come out of His Grace, His Compassion.... To contact God, one has to open his eyes and serve his brother man. The greatest joy springs from the utmost sacrifice. It is the utmost fulfillment. Giving is gaining.

...The whole world is today in the throes of anxiety and fear. But I assure you that very soon the dark clouds will be scattered and you will witness a happy era all over the world. Right will be restored and evil put down. Your duty is to yearn for the attainment of the consciousness of the One behind all this apparent multiplicity. Be centers of love, compassion, service, mutual tolerance, and be happy—very, very happy.

--Sathya Sai Baba
Sathya Sai Speaks, Vol. VII, Chap. 86

Chapter Fourteen

OUR EXEMPLAR

When Swami tells us to be "centers of love, compassion, service, mutual tolerance, and be happy--very, very happy," He is telling us to be like Him. He exemplifies each of these so beautifully in His daily actions. I can recall my human father telling me, "Don't do as I do; do as I say." The conflict and confusion this instruction aroused in me is now being carefully eliminated by my Divine Guru, my Heavenly Father. His acts are always clear examples of his teachings.

Upon our arrival in Kodaikanal, Swami showed His compassion and His happiness to us very clearly. As we had been in the caravan of cars which had followed Him from Brindavan, we were present when He gave the first darshan of 1994 in the beautiful hilltop home overlooking the lake.

On the first day, April 6, 1994, As He came out on the veranda and walked down the stairs toward the men, He went almost directly to where Raye was sitting. He looked down at him with the love of a thousand mothers, saying, "You've been very, very sick. I know, I know. What is your program?" Raye held up four fingers, and Swami asked, "Four weeks?" Raye answered, "No, Swami, four months." Then with a radiant smile, Swami said, "Very, very good, very happy." He took a letter Raye had written Him, and Raye was in perfect bliss.

I was sitting in the chair section in the row closest to Swami's walkway. When He came to the foot of the stairs, He appeared to be ready to go on up to the second floor. However, He looked over at me, gave a smile of recognition, and walked toward me. With a look of innocent delight, like that of an angelic child, He said with glee, "Your husband is there," and pointed toward the men's section. He accepted the letters I had brought from the States, then He took the first eleven chapters of this book, held it in His hand for several seconds, reading, "Life is Love." Then He gently handed it back to me saying, "You keep." My heart overflowed with love and gratitude for His Grace.

On the following day, He again came to Raye. This time He asked, "Where is wife?" Raye said, "Over there, Swami," pointing toward the ladies' side. Swami then replied, "Very happy, very happy!"

When I had arrived in darshan that morning, all of the chairs were taken. I sat on the ground in front of the chairs. When Swami came where I was, He asked with an almost mischievous, little-boy grin, "Husband is here?" I replied, "Oh, yes, Swami. We love You and we thank You. Padnamaskar, please, Swami?" He replied, "Yes, yes, do." I held on to His precious feet then as long as I dared. He waited patiently. When I released those beautiful soft little feet, He still stood there for another moment. I reached up toward Him, then, and He took my hand, holding it for only a few seconds.

The next day He again expressed His happiness to Raye. On this morning, however, I had reverted to the wheelchair. I was resigned to being placed in the back corner, as far away from Baba as it is possible to get in that section. When that's exactly where I was put, I was at peace. Then a few drops of rain fell, signaling the possibility of a downpour. The chair people were given a choice--they could either stay where they were or move under cover. Everyone in my row elected to go for cover, leaving me in the front row! Thus it was that, once again, Swami was able to come where I was.

When He did, He played the word game with me, which game I almost consistently lose. He asked, "Where is your bender?" When I looked blank, He repeated the question. In the face of my silence, He asked the same question for the third time. I was still speechless. Then He said, "Where is your husband?" pronouncing the word "husband" very clearly. Relieved, I pointed to the men's side and said, "He's here, Swami, due to Your healing him." At that point, I completely blissed out. I was not localized in space, time, or body. Many people told me later that Swami tapped me twice on the head, but I was unaware of it at the time.

Although He has told us before, "Husband--has bended," my mind simply will not come up with such information when my heart is so full of His Presence. I've never been totally sure what He means when He uses this play on words. I hope that He doesn't mean that the husband has bent to the wife's will. Although that might have been true on certain occasions in the past, in this case, I feel fairly certain that it meant that Raye had bent to the Divine Will.

At any rate, the interaction with Swami, whatever He says, produces bliss on the part of the devotee.

He communicates Himself, and He is the embodiment of bliss. As He has said, "Only the spring of bliss can confer bliss." (**Sathya Sai Speaks XI,** Chap. 1, p. 2) For the thirty days during which we were in Kodaikanal, we were almost constantly in bliss. His sweet Krishna Self gave us the opportunity to see Him twice daily. He frequently touched our hands or our heads, and often spoke words which reassured us of His love and care.

Writing of the experience, S. Sampath said in the June 1994 issue of **Sanathana Sarathi:**

> Over a whole month, day after day in Kodaikanal, Bhagavan took infinite trouble to inculcate in the minds of those who were privileged to be with Him a deep understanding of Love and the importance of Awareness, Purity, Selflessness, and Divinity. Bhagavan's message is for the whole of humanity, overriding religions, caste, creed, sex, color, and all such divisive factors. The small band of people, blessed by Bhagavan to be close to His Lotus Feet for thirty days, have a God-ordained obligation to be the torchbearers of His effulgent Divine message.

Chapter Fifteen

THE SERVICE OF GOOD DEEDS

Baba's message to the world includes guidelines for conduct which will assist us in our efforts to gain the ultimate victory over birth and death. He says:

> *I have told you often that besides revering your parents, your teachers, and your elders, you also have to revere your deeds. Deeds elevate us or drag us down; they chain us to both birth and death, or they deliver us from the chain. They result in joy or grief, prosperity or poverty, gain or loss, pleasure or pain. You must realize that your enthusiasm or despair, success or failure, are but the consequences of your actions.... In every deed or act, God is present as the Invisible Motivator; in every minute thing that you handle or manipulate, God is present as the Inner Core. So, always try to elevate yourselves by doing good, speaking good, seeking good, and having the good of others in mind.*
>
> --**Sathya Sai Speaks, Vol. X,** Chap. 25

Jesus told his disciples that "The kingdom of heaven is like unto leaven which a woman took and hid in three measures of meal until the whole was leavened." (**Holy Bible,** Matt. 13:33) The meaning of this parable becomes clear when we see evidence that Baba's teachings are gently raising the consciousness of all mankind, inspiring individuals to perform deeds which will bless others, with no thought of any return for themselves.

An article entitled "The Kindness Revolution" appeared in the **Ladies Home Journal** of March, 1993. The lead paragraph reads: "It all started in California, naturally. In 1983, San Francisco artist Anne Herbert decided that doing unexpected favors for strangers could help make the world a better place. Her idea to engage in 'Random Acts of Kindness' started popping up in newspapers, on billboards, pins, and bumper stickers. Soon there were reports of people doing such things as paying the toll for cars behind them at toll plazas, or fixing up elderly couples' rundown houses. Last year, a group of 'kindness practitioners' got together to share their stories."

The stories include one about a boy who had saved his money for months in order to buy an expensive baseball mitt. When he finally came to the store with his shoebox full of nickels, quarters, and dimes, the total came to $19.95. The manager realized that the actual price of the mitt, which was $79.95, had become slightly smudged and that a desperately hopeful seven-year-old could easily imagine it to be $19.95. Therefore, he smiled, wrapped the mitt, and gave it to the boy.

Others tell of the "coffee angel" who prepaid for the next twenty customers who ordered coffee at a small restaurant which caters to working people; the kind fellow-workers who kept fresh flowers on the desk of a depressed employee; and the San Francisco market owner who regularly takes over for frightened motorists as they attempt to drive up and over the very steep hill on which his store is located.

There is no question that each of these deeds was divinely inspired. But no inspiration could equal that which the devotees at Kodaikanal felt when they witnessed the Lord in form, our own beloved Swami, demonstrate to all present for darshan one lovely day, the essence of this teaching.

There was a lady sitting on a rock ledge which was between the driveway and the covered area. She was alone there, perhaps having arrived late. There was no walkway available for Swami to go to her. Between where she sat and the carpet which was spread out for Swami to walk on, there was only an uncleared area which was quite rocky. Normally there would have been no need for anyone to walk there.

However, on this morning, when Swami came to the point nearest to the lady on the wall, she held out some letters which she seemed to wish urgently to give Him. She appealed to Him to allow her to come to Him to hand Him the letters. However, He held up His hand, indicating that she was not to get up. Then, to the chagrin of those watching, He left the carpet and walked across the sharp rocks which separated them. He sweetly accepted the letters which she offered, then returned across the rocky area to continue gracing other devotees with His nearness.

Although it would not have been humanly possible to have made that trip across the rocks without being cut and bruised, there was no sign that

He even was aware of the many stones which passed under His feet. His selfless deed caused His message to become deeply engraved in our hearts: put others' welfare before your own, and you will be lifted up.

* * * * * * * * *

The good that you do will guard you; have that faith rooted in your mind.

Sathya Sai Speaks, Vol. IX, Chap. 2

Treat everyone as the embodiment of the Divine which you worship; treat every word and deed of yours as an offering to the Lord whom you adore. Then you can escape the taint of envy or malice, falsehood or greed, anger or egotism.

Sathya Sai Speaks, Vol. VII, Chap. 62

Chapter Sixteen

"I WILL GIVE"

When Swami left Kodaikanal on May 4, we felt a slight pang that the blessed visit was over. He had given so much to so many. What would it be like now in Brindavan? We again joined the caravan of cars following Swami and felt great joy when our car was close to His.

Arriving in Brindavan in the evening, we prayed that He might see fit to put us up in His Guest House. After a long wait, we were finally told that we had been assigned to room A-4. Was it only a coincidence that the number is the same as our apartment in Puttaparthi? How can we fathom Swami's purposes? We rejoiced to know that the number 4 is the name for God among some peoples, thanked Swami for His Grace, and promptly went to sleep.

The next morning when I went to darshan I was faced with a difficult decision. My options were: to sit on the built-in bench, which was, at that time, much too high for comfort; to sit on the floor in the fourth block, causing extra work for those who had to help me up and down; or to stay in the wheelchair and be placed against the back railing where the chances of ever having any interaction with Swami were slim indeed. I was still pondering which choice would be best when a lovely lady devotee whom I have met several times in Puttaparthi called to me to sit by her on the bench. That seemed to be the answer for me, and so I took my place cn the bench. My feet wouldn't touch the floor and the extremely hot morning sun burned my back, but I would have a chance that Swami might come near. After all, this is the Kali Yuga, and getting close to the Avatar was never intended to be easy.

Thus it was that on May 7, Swami came out the gate of the compound, entered the first arch, and walked along by the bench until He came to where I was. "How long are you staying?" He asked. I replied, "May we have permission to stay for Summer Course, Swami?" He replied, "Yes, yes, yes. You and husband come inside."

I felt no limitation or hesitation whatsoever. The thought of getting the wheelchair didn't even occur to me. I walked through the gate to the compound and sat down on the bench to wait for Swami to return. The Seva Dal carefully seated us, ladies on the left and gents on the right. Raye was sitting on the bench closest to the gate and so, when Swami entered the gate, He approached Raye and asked, "Where is your wife? Why are you not sitting with her? Your wife is your life!" Then he went up the ramp and disappeared inside.

A moment later, He came to the door and signaled us to come in. As there were a number of ladies, only two gents, and a student, the ladies sat on Swami's left, filling the area. I sat on the floor at the back with no difficulty getting down at all. My body responded to the command to sit as if the legs were perfect and were no more than eighteen years old! However, when Swami entered and saw me on the floor, He said, "Sit on the couch." So I sprang to my feet with none of the usual struggle and sat on the very comfortable sofa.

After all of the devotees were seated, Swami settled in His chair, looked at me, and asked, "Where is Sai Baba?" I touched my hand to my heart and replied, "In my heart, Swami." His quick rejoinder was, "Then what are you doing here?" I responded, "I so love to be with the Form, Swami." And He said, "Aaah, the Form."

Then He asked, "What is the name of your new book?" I replied, "Life Is Love, Enjoy It!" He repeated the name and then asked me, "How is it?" I replied, "I pray that it is to Your liking, Swami." Raye removed a copy from his bag and handed it to Him. Swami opened it to the first page, looked at the picture of the three of us and said, "Drawing." I said, "Yes, Swami, it is a drawing done from the photograph taken in the interview room at Prasanthi Nilayam in February, '93. He then glanced through the book and commented that the black and white pictures were too dark. They certainly were! I said that I would see to it that the black and white prints are properly shaded when the book comes from the printer.

It had been my plan to have a good black pen with me when we asked Swami to sign the book. However, I had been totally without hope that He would call that morning, and so I had brought none of the things that I had intended to have with me if and when I was called for the precious interview. Raye offered his pen, which had blue ink, and Swami signed in His beautiful handwriting, "With love, Baba."

The blue ink looks delightful--so much prettier than the black would have been--since He signed right under the "drawing." That page will be in color and the blue will show up nicely. It also answered my concern that He might not approve it simply because it was a drawing. His approval gave me the necessary green light to finish the book and take it to the printer.

The next question was addressed to Raye. He asked, "What do you want?" Raye replied, "Liberation, Swami." This was a first for Raye. He had always previously said that he had no desire for liberation, that he would be happy to reincarnate in order to serve others. The Lord of the Universe, the One who has the power to grant liberation, looked up toward and beyond the ceiling, moving His head slightly from side to side as if He were reading. Then He replied, "I will give--in one minute." For an instant I thought that He meant that He would give Raye liberation one minute later. However, I quickly realized that He had meant that He would give him liberation and that--when the time came--it would be instant, in one minute. We were both so overcome with love and devotion that we could not have spoken another word. Swami knew that, as He knows everything, and turned away to give His love and attention to the others in the room.

He manifested a ring with an image of Himself on it, asking one of the ladies whether or not she wanted Sai Baba. She replied, "Yes, Sai Baba," but even I noticed the lack of conviction in her voice. Baba then took the ring, blew on it, and changed the image to Jesus. The lady seemed to be very happy with the picture of Jesus.

He waved His hand again, producing another ring. This time He got up from His chair without opening His hand, came to where I was, then revealed a ring and placed it on my index finger. As my hands were a little moist and swollen from the heat, the ring did not go all the way on easily. (It now fits my index finger perfectly.) He removed it and placed it on my fourth finger, right hand. To my astonishment and delight, it was a silver ring with an embossed image of Shirdi Sai. Baba hadn't asked me what I wanted. Obviously He knew everything. In my time of sorrow, He had comforted me in His Shirdi form, and He knew how thrilled I would be to have His image in that form on my finger.

In addition to His blessing my newly established relationship with Shirdi Sai, He also knew that prior to leaving on this trip, I had expressed the wish to Raye that Baba would make me another ring, but I qualified that by adding, "Only, however, if He doesn't take my present ring. I love it with its golden image of Sathya Sai, and I don't want it changed." He gives and gives, fulfilling our desires, and always bringing us closer to union with Him.

Then Swami asked me, "How many kilos do you weigh?" I thought He was going to fuss at me again for being too fat, but I answered bravely, "I don't know in kilos, Swami, but I weigh about 250 lbs." Then He spoke to the group, saying, "She used to be as big as a roadroller," illustrating by holding His hands wide apart, "but now she looks good." Later, as we discussed the interview with five of the other ladies present, they firmly stated that Baba had also said, "Now she's just a little girl." I didn't hear the words, but I love them. I would be so grateful to become like a little child and be worthy to enter the kingdom of heaven.

Actually, the interview room is as near the kingdom of heaven as we'll ever get on this earth! Swami did not ask Raye to remove His big ring this time, as He has so often done, but He took Raye's hand and held it up. Showing the group the pictures of Himself, Jesus, Shirdi, and the Om sign, as well as a jeweled cross which Raye had just added to commemorate Swami's making a cross over the ring on a previous occasion, Swami said laughingly, "He wants it all!"

Then He asked Raye and me to come inside to the private interview room. Again, I easily sat on the floor at His left. When He sat down, I kissed His precious feet, lingering with my lips on His big toes. What a glorious privilege --a priceless gift--and to think that there was a time which I was so unaware of His glory and majesty that I thought such an act to be degrading.

When I returned to the world of time and space, Raye was telling Swami that He would like to live in India and work for Him. Having entered this conversation in the middle, I somehow got the impression that Raye was asking to work for Baba in Brindavan. So I blurted out "Prasanthi Nilayam." Swami looked at me briefly and said, "Yes." Then He turned back to Raye, saying, "I will give you a <u>good</u> job, and I will give you a place in Brindavan, too." My mind could hardly absorb the enormity of this blessing. While I was in bliss, Raye and Baba discussed Raye's present work, selling real estate, showing property, etc. He asked Raye again, "You want to live in India?" and Raye assured Him that he did.

Earlier, in the outer room, Swami had said to Raye, "Wife fights with you--like yesterday in the room--but don't worry, it's just reaction. She has a good heart." Raye agreed with Swami by saying, "Yes, she has a big heart." But Swami, as He so often does, declined the terminology which had been used and, showing again His well-developed sense of humor, replied, "No! Not big heart! With big heart you have to go to the hospital!"

While they were debating "good" versus "big," I was feeling deep regret and questioning why I had been so irritable recently. It seemed to me that in Kodai, if I wasn't in darshan, I was either sleeping or finding fault with someone. I had said several times, "I'm just not myself at all." So, when Swami turned to me saying, "You've been having some depression. In Kodaikanal, you kept thinking, 'Swami isn't going to see me. Why won't He talk to me?'" At this point I dissolved into tears, begging Him to please help me be better. He stroked my head, telling me not to cry, assuring me that all would be all right. When He had said that He would give us a place in Brindavan, I had expressed my gratitude by saying that I had always found it difficult to manage in Brindavan, and He assured me that all would be all right in that situation also.

Back in the outer room, Swami asked me, "How's your boy?" For some reason, I thought He was referring to Raye, and I answered, "Very good." Swami reacted in surprise and disbelief, "Very good?!!!" I realized later that He was probably asking about my son. Humanly, my son is "very good." He is a hard worker, makes an excellent living for his family, and he is a practicing Christian. As far as my relationship with him, however, it is nonexistent. He still thinks I'm a lost soul in that I'm worshiping Baba instead of Jesus. Perhaps I'll get the chance to talk to Swami about it again sometime. I am always comforted by remembering that He told me years ago that "e-ven-tu-ally it will all come right."

As the interview was nearing its end, I asked Swami if we might have a robe for a new Center near us in USA. He replied, "I will give." Raye, also thinking of the new Center, asked, "Swami, may I have your hankie?" Swami said, "Kerchief? Yes, take." Raye was next to His chair, and Swami was distributing vibhuti, so he reached up, took one of the handkerchiefs, then reached for the other one. Swami said, "Not two!" and we all laughed. We remembered Him saying, "He wants it all!" when He referred to Raye's ring. And it also seemed a perfect example of the way we all feel about Swami, we always want more.

As we all reluctantly began to prepare to leave, Raye and I were among the last to go. Suddenly it became apparent that one lady who had sat on the floor was having great difficulty getting up. Raye and Swami both instantly moved to her aid. Raye took her right arm, and Swami, her left, and together they had her on her feet in a moment. The last two to leave the room were Raye and Swami. They walked out chatting like old chums, and Swami asked Raye for the third time, "You want to live in India?" and, for the third time, Raye replied, "Yes."

That same day, before afternoon bhajans, dear Barbara Henderson came to our room. She brought a simple stool about six inches tall and asked, "Could you use this under your feet at darshan? I think it would take the pressure off your knees and allow the blood to circulate better in your legs." Swami had assured me that morning that He would make it easier for me in Brindavan, and here was His instrument, Barbara, fulfilling that promise. I gratefully accepted the little stool and took it with me every day until, within the next two months, the high benches were removed and replaced with lower ones.

At afternoon bhajans, another devotee presented me with the gift of the book **Sathya Sai's Amrita Varshini** (Nectarine Showers) by Sudha Aditya. She particularly drew my attention to the chapter entitled "The Dark Period." The text quotes Baba as having said that every aspirant goes through these dark periods, which are in fact periods of maturing. These periods do not occur at the beginning of the sadhaka's path. It is about at the middle of the path that the real process of learning begins. "During your sadhana you have undergone various experiences and learned many things. All these facts have to be assimilated by the inner spirit, analyzed and converted into knowledge and wisdom....For example, what happens after you have eaten a meal? The food has the be absorbed, digested, and assimilated by the system. You cannot see the process of digestion and assimilation, but they are going on in the body. It is the same in the case of spiritual food also. You read religious books, listen to bhajans and discourses, take part in satsang sessions, practise sadhana and dhyana. All these are food for the spirit within. The spiritual food has to be absorbed, digested, and assimilated by the inner self. The end result of this process is spiritual, mental and emotional growth, and maturity....The periods of maturing in a sadhaka's life are similar to the plateaus. When the darkness lifts and light breaks, you will emerge re-vitalized and re-invigorated, ready to move to greater heights." (pp. 16-19)

> *You must have heard of people seeking liberation and getting liberation, and many may be under the impression that it is some rare honor that only a few secure, or that it is some area like paradise, or a colony of the elect, or a height that only a few heroic souls can finally attain. No! Liberation is something which all must achieve, whether they are heroic or not. Even those who deny its existence will ultimately realize it. For, everyone is seeking liberation when he seeks joy and peace; and who does not seek joy and peace? When you have lasting joy and lasting peace, you are liberated. Tired of temporary joys and transient peace, man will at last seek to know the secret of permanent joy and peace, that is to say, liberation.*
>
> *If only men knew the path to permanent joy and peace, they would not wander distracted among the bylanes of sensual pleasure. Just as the joy felt in dreams disappears when you wake up, the joy felt in the waking stage disappears when you awake to higher awareness (jnana). So, the Upanishads say, "Get up! Arise! Awake! Time is fleeting*

fast. While the moment is available, put it to the best of uses; the awareness of the Divine is all. When you die, you must die, not like a tree, a beast, or a worm, but like a man who realizes himself to be Divine (Madhava). That is proper consummation of all the years that you spend in human form.

Sathya Sai Baba
Voice of the Avatar, Vol. I

The nine steps in the pilgrimage of man towards God along the path of dedication and surrender are 1) developing a desire to listen to the glory and grandeur of the handiwork of God and of the various awe-inspiring manifestations of Divinity. This is the starting point. It is by hearing about the Lord again and again, that we can transform ourselves into Divinity. 2) Singing about the Lord, in praise of His magnificence and manifold exploits. 3) Dwelling on the Lord in the mind, reveling in the contemplation of His beauty, majesty, and compassion. 4) Entering upon the worship of the Lord by honoring the feet. 5) This develops into a total propitiation of the Lord and systematic worship in which the aspirant gets inner satisfaction and inspiration. 6) The aspirant begins to see the favorite Form of God, which he likes to worship, in all beings and all objects, wherever he turns, and so he develops an attitude of reverence towards nature and all life. 7) Established in this bent of mind, he becomes the devoted servant of all, with no sense of superiority or inferiority. This is a vital step, which presages great spiritual success. 8) This takes the seeker so near the Lord that he feels himself to be the confidant and comrade, the companion and friend, the sharer of God's power and pity, of God's triumphs and achievements, as did Arjuna to Krishna. 9) As can be inferred, this is the prelude to the final step of total surrender, yielding fully to the Will of the Lord which the seeker knows through his own purified intuition.

Sathya Sai Baba
Sathya Sai Speaks, Vol. VII, Chap. 40

Chapter Seventeen

PROPERTY RIGHTS

May had been a month of beautiful, long, lovely darshans. There were many occasions on which Swami had smiled, spoken, and/or touched the members of our group during darshan. The number had dwindled down to nine. Most of the original thirty-two devotees who had traveled together from the States had long since had to return. The remaining nine were still praying for interview.

On May 27, I decided that I would perform a sadhana which I had attempted several times before and failed. It is to read the book about Shirdi Baba, **Shri Sai Satcharita,** completely through from the first page to the last in seven days. It is said that one may gain a boon if one successfully imbibes all of the wonderful stories about Shirdi Sai in the space of one week. The boon for which I asked as I performed this ritual was that our group be granted an interview.

It was not easy to keep reading. The stories are so fascinating and the lessons so profound that the temptation is to ponder them, talk about them, and generally dawdle over the reading. Obviously, pondering Truth has great advantages, but evidently this particular ritual is designed to so pile truth on top of truth that nothing remains in consciousness but Truth.

Because Swami had graced Patricia Boyce, a member of our group, and me, as well as others, on several occasions by placing His hand on our heads, I could not have been more delighted when I came to the following passages in **Shri Sai Satcharita:**

"Efficacy of the Touch of the Guru's Hand

"Where Real or Sad-Guru is the helmsman, he is sure to carry us safely and easily beyond the worldly ocean. The word Sadguru brings to mind Sai Baba. He appears to me, as if standing before me, and applying Udi (sacred ashes) to my forehead and placing His hand of blessing on my head. Then joy fills my heart and love overflows through my eyes. Wonderful is the power of the touch of the Guru's hand. The subtle body (consisting of thoughts and desires), which cannot be burned by world-dissolving fire, is destroyed by the mere touch of the Guru's hand, and the sins of many past births are cleansed and washed away."

Shri Sai Satcharita, p. 31
by Nagesh Vasudev Gunaji, B.A., LL.B.

On page 212, the author again refers to the same subject, saying:

"Blessed is Shri Sai Samartha, Who gives instructions in both temporal and spiritual matters to His devotees and makes them happy by enabling them to achieve the goals of their lives, Who, when He places His hand on their heads, transfers His powers to them, thus destroying the sense of differentiation and enabling them to attain the Unattainable Thing."

With such enlightening and encouraging information coming on every page, I could hardly put the book down. Thus it was that I finished the final pages on June 2 at 8:55 p.m., just five minutes before "lights out." It was on that day also that Ilesha, another of our group members, had a dream in which Baba granted us an interview.

On the following morning, June 3, Raye went to his assigned block for morning darshan. The Seva Dal, who had frequently seated him behind the post, told him on this morning that there was no room for him at all. He was to go back to the next block. Raye patiently and obediently did as he was told. Once again, we were shown that it makes no difference at all where you are seated, when Swami wants you, He will find you wherever you are.

When Swami came that morning, He entered by the door of the Shanti Vedika, walked across the stage to the men's side, down the stairs, past the students, past the block where Raye had not been allowed to sit, and on to the next block. He walked directly to where Raye was and asked, "How many in your group?" Raye replied, "Nine, Swami," and Our Beloved Lord said, "Go."

When I saw Raye getting up and holding up his scarf, I got up promptly. It was my intention to again walk through the gate to the compound without using the wheelchair. I did so with no difficulty at all. Once more I was sitting in that beautiful garden, in Baba's compound, waiting to ascend the ramp to the interview room.

While waiting for Swami to come from darshan, my heart was singing, "He gave the boon!" Ilesha was overjoyed that her dream had come true. Dear Ilesha felt such love for Swami that she had gotten slightly carried away one day in darshan. When He had already passed her, and had stopped to speak to me, she was so overcome by her love for Him that she stretched out her hand and touched Him only slightly on His elbow. He didn't seem to notice, but the Seva Dals did. She was relegated to the very back row as punishment for touching Swami as He passed in Darshan.

Her reaction was like Raye's. She had patiently and obediently sat in the back as she had been told to do. Now she would be sitting at Swami's feet. At last He came, and we all went inside. This time I made no effort to sit on the floor. I sat on the end of the couch as far away from the men as possible. However, there were more men in this interview than there had been in our first one, so I appeared to be sitting on the men's side. Swami did not let this go unnoticed. When He came in He looked at me and said, "Men's side?" But He said nothing further, evidently feeling that it would be all right for me to remain there.

Sitting on the floor at Swami's left were Ilesha and Patricia. I would like to introduce you to them, using interviews which they gave Susan Caffery and which she printed in "The Overseas Observer."

"Patricia Boyce is from Seattle, Washington, USA. She lived most of her life as a devout Catholic and is the mother of eight. She says that she was always quite serious about her religion. From childhood, she felt particularly close to God. She found out about Swami in 1979.

"The doctor told Patricia when she was 28 that she was legally blind. It was a complete shock, as she didn't know that there was anything really wrong with her eyes. She was slowly losing her peripheral vision. But when she heard the news from the doctor, she also heard a message within. God said, 'This is for My purpose. This is not a burden for you to bear, and you will never suffer.' She wasn't afraid, for she trusted the God within her heart.

"In 1982, Swami told her in an interview, 'One week of sadhana--then vision.' When the other devotees heard that, they were sure that her sight would be restored. But Patricia hoped that it would be inner-sight which she would receive. It was.

"Patricia says, 'My eyes aren't good now. I can't see Baba at all. But I have inner vision. I see Him inside, and He talks to me.' In [this] interview, in response to Patricia's thanking Swami for her inner sight, Baba confirmed that grace by saying, 'Yes, very good inner vision.'

"We asked if her inner-sight included clairvoyance. 'I know that I know all that I need to know. I don't want those other things. I am very clear about the God that I am. I totally trust my inner self. I don't see Baba when He comes out to give darshan, but I feel His presence, and my friend Ilesha describes everything to me. I am aware of so much grace, and I feel the Angels around me all the time.'

"Because of God's inner message to Patricia that her condition was given to serve His purpose and because of her total trust in her inner Self--even though this is her first trip to Baba in which she cannot see at all, she made the journey alone, totally trusting in His grace.

"Patricia hopes that sharing her story with others will give them courage and strength, knowing that whatever form of darkness they may be faced with, they may also know that God's grace is there for them. 'Just trust in Him,' she says. 'Baba always provides.'"

And the interview with Ilesha reads:

"These two ladies [Ilesha and Patricia] have established a wonderful connection here in India. Ilesha is temporarily on crutches [due to an injury to her foot which occured just before leaving the States], and Patricia carries a white cane. Ilesha has guided Patricia so sweetly and carefully for the past few weeks, giving all of her time and attention to this lady whom she had never seen before. She has been rewarded by Patricia's light, wisdom, and love, which are a true gift to any friend.

"During the interview, gesturing them into the private room, Swami said, 'The blind and the lame, go inside.' As they walked into the room, Ilesha hopped on one leg, not wishing to use her crutches. Swami laughed and said, 'Pogo dancing.'

"Swami had given a ring to Patricia in 1985, and she had used it to help others. She even allowed them to keep it for awhile if they needed it for health purposes. Finally, it broke in half, and Patricia had brought it with her to this interview. Ilesha held Patricia's hand out toward Swami, offering Him the ring. He held it for a long time. Then He gave the half with His picture on it to Ilesha. 'Keep it,' the beautiful Lord said. 'Put it in your purse.' Ilesha said that she didn't have a purse, pointing to her 'fanny pack.' Swami said, 'Put it there and zip it up. Keep it.'

"Then the Lord took the other half of the ring and held it lightly in His fingers. 'What is this?' He asked. 'Silver, Swami,' everyone said. Then He blew on it and changed it to a gold ring with three diamonds. Ilesha took Patricia's hand and held it up toward Swami. But, instead, the Lord slipped the ring on Ilesha's hand, which was outstretched so unselfishly to help her friend. What a wonderful teaching.

"Later, He told Ilesha, 'I will give you a very good husband!' and He snapped His fingers loudly twice."

I don't think that I was the only one who wondered what Swami's purpose might be in taking Patricia's ring and giving it to Ilesha. However, Patricia herself seemed to find only joy in the entire procedure. It was a source of great happiness to me to see Ilesha receiving such an abundance of Swami's grace, due to the fact that she had exercised such equanimity in the difficult situation which had resulted from her touching Him. I was totally confident that Swami's action was perfect, but I could not at first understand its meaning. However, the interview went on and I put aside my questions, thinking, "I'll ponder that tomorrow."

Swami was now giving His attention to an Indian couple, speaking to them in Telegu. I realized that I had seen the lady before. On December 23, 1989, Swami had granted us an interview in Puttaparthi. He had also called the lady who was now in this interview. Baba had carried on a long conversation with her in Telegu. There were just enough words in English for us to understand that the lady's husband was in a hospital for the purpose of having heart bypass surgery. Baba manifested a gold vibhuti box for her, which we presumed contained vibhuti for herself and her husband. Then with a quick wave of His hand, He created a round, white tablet, showed it to the group, and said, "This is for operation. It's chloroform--like chloroform." He wrapped the tablet in a piece of paper and told the wife that she should give it to her husband before the operation.

It was, therefore, very rewarding to us to find that the lady and a handsome, healthy gentleman were in this interview. Five years had passed since we had seen a very unhappy lady, pleading with Baba for His help. Although we had no way to know what had happened in the intervening period, obviously, the lady was now very happy. Baba carried on a lively conversation with the couple in Telegu and, after the interview, allowed a picture to be taken of Himself with them.

Then Swami told Raye and me to go into the inner room. This time I had all of my materials with me. I had brought a children's book and an American translation of **Geetha Vahini** with me in hope of receiving His direction in regard to publishing them. He gave His loving attention to both of the books, signing each of them with His love. Then Raye asked Him, "When shall we return to India, Swami?" and His reply indicated that we could return as soon as all of our affairs were in order in the United States. Raye, then, held out another copy of the first eleven chapters of this book, asking Swami if He would sign on

"How many in your group?"

the title page. He took the book, stood up, and said, "I will sign it outside."

When we were again seated in the outer room, and Swami had placed the little book on the arm of His chair, He stood up and began to distribute vibhuti. Knowing quite well that this signaled the end of the interview, I got out the picture of Swami which I hoped to use on the cover of the book, and a pen with which He might sign it if He so willed.

At this point, He walked back to His chair, picked up our little eleven chapters and tossed it to an Indian gentleman sitting beside Raye. When Swami returned to the distribution of vibhuti packets, Raye gave the Indian gentleman a pen, asking that when Swami came would he please hold up the book for Swami to sign it on the title page. Swami came, the gentleman asked, and Swami very sweetly signed it on both the title page and the picture page, also dating it. When He came to me, He graciously signed the picture for the cover of the book and gave me a double handful of vibhuti packets.

Our little taste of heaven was over. We went down the ramp with a sigh. Upon reaching the garden, Raye asked the Indian gentleman for the book. He clutched it to him, saying, "No, Swami gave it to me." Raye was in shock. That thought had obviously not struck him before. At that moment, I felt the need to intervene. I stepped up to the gentleman, saying, "I understand how you feel. Would you please be kind enough to just have Xerox copies made of the pages with the signatures and give them to us." He agreed to do so, and we watched as our little book with the two precious signatures disappeared into the crowd.

Now I had even greater incentive to find an answer to the questions, "Why did He give Patricia's ring to Ilesha?" and "Why did He sign our book and give it to someone else?" After considerable time spent pondering, the following quotation came as the answer.

> *What is the sum and substance of all these discourses? It is that man has to give up his pursuit of sensory objects if he seeks lasting peace and joy. Material wealth brings along with it, not only joy but grief. Accumulation of riches, multiplication of wants—these lead only to alternation between joy and grief. Attachment is the root of both joy and grief; detachment is the savior. A millionaire pays income tax with tears in his eyes; the Headmaster joyfully gives up the furniture and laboratory appliances of his school when he is transferred to some other place. Why? Because the Headmaster knows that he is only the caretaker, not the owner. He is not attached to those articles; he knows that they belong to the Government. So, too, feel that your family, your house, your fields, your car, are all the Lord's property and that you are only the trustee; be ready to give them up without a murmur, at a moment's notice.*

Sathya Sai Baba
Sathya Sai Speaks, Vol. IV, Chap. 16

If I can understand this teaching and live by it, it will certainly be of assistance when I go back to the States and let go of a lifetime accumulation of things. All of the things I've called "mine," do in fact belong to God. I have been the caretaker. Now I will release them to Him, and Swami can assign as caretaker whomsoever He wills.

These are two of Raye's and my favorite bhajans. We have sung them many times, assigning everything to God. But when it comes to one of Baba's precious manifestations or His signature, we tend to slip up.

LORD, TAKE MY HAND

Lord, take my hand.
Guide me through this day.
Fill my heart with love.
Please show me the way.

Lord, hear my prayer
That I may never stray.
Heal my body, mind, and soul.
Hear me as I pray.

Lord, take my heart.
Soften it today.
Cleanse my thoughts, my words, my deeds,
Purifying me this way.

Lord, take my life.
Let Thy will be done.
Fill me full of grace
Until we merge as One.

SURRENDER TO THE LORD

(To the tune of Ganesha Sharanam)

Surrender to the Lord, to the Lord, surrender.
Take my love in fullness of devotion to Thee, Oh, Lord.
Take my hands and let them work incessantly for Thee, Oh, Lord.
Take my soul and let it be merged in One with Thee, O Lord.

Surrender to the Lord, to the Lord, surrender.
Take my mind and let it be in tune with Thee, Oh, Lord.
Oh, take my everything; let me be Your instrument.
Take my soul and let it be merged in One with Thee, O Lord.

Chapter Eighteen

HE ANSWERS PRAYERS

It was on a warm, sunny day, June 5, that the President of India came to Brindavan for a visit with Swami. Afterwards, he spoke to all of us, referring to Baba as an Acharya. He gave the definition of "Acharya" as 'one who doesn't teach by words but by example." I thought to myself, "So, the President of the country has noticed that, too!"

At that moment, my body suddenly felt icy cold and began to shake. I made an all-out effort to remain still, but to no avail. I was shaking uncontrollably from head to toe. Two Seva Dals quickly came to get me out of the mass of devotees and back to my room. From the men's side, Raye saw what was happening, and he came to the room also. All of the sheets and bedspreads were put over me, and, I think, some shawls also. Finally warmth began to creep back into my body. With regret that I was missing Swami's discourse, I fell asleep.

When I awakened in the morning, I saw--to my distress--that during the night my right leg had swollen to double its size. It was dark red and extremely hot. There had been a small spot on my right foot a few days ago, but with the help of several friends, it had been well cared for and was now healed. What was going on? I seemed to have some fever. My stomach was in great pain. Obviously, I couldn't go to darshan in this condition.

Raye assessed the situation and said, "Get ready. I'm taking you to the Apollo Hospital." We had heard many devotees speak of the fine care they had received there in time of need. Swami had dedicated this state-of-the-art hospital on June 3, 1991, just three years, three days ago. I put up as much resistance as I could muster, which wasn't very much. Then remembering how many times Swami had told me to surrender to the wishes of my husband, I gave in and meekly got into the car to be taken to Bangalore.

However, arriving in the emergency room, I obviously was still not completely surrendered to the whole procedure. When the doctor on duty said that I should be admitted, I asked for a private room, thinking, "Whatever happens, I will need some privacy in order to be in the silence, to do my sadhana, to pray to Swami."

Although the excruciating pain in my stomach subsided quickly, it was clear from the beginning that no stone would be left unturned until all contributing factors to my physical distress were located and eliminated. Of course, I was immediately put on regular doses of antibiotics to combat the massive infection in my leg. A blood test revealed that the blood sugar was elevated, thus insulin shots were begun at once. A chest X-ray was made, and I was put on steam inhalation therapy three or four times a day. But it was ultra sound which confirmed the suspicion already held by my doctor that a growth was present in the right lower abdominal wall. This growth seemed to be pressing on the nerves and veins of the right leg, and I overheard the doctor saying that it seemed almost inevitable that the growth was malignant.

As my admitting doctor was an extremely busy surgeon, he had to make time between surgeries to explain the situation to Raye and me. He said that the growth which showed up in the ultra sound pictures and was clearly visible in the CT Scan was undoubtedly the major underlying factor in the problem with the leg. The growth would have to be surgically removed. However, it was impossible to do the operation until the infection in the leg was completely cleared up.

And so the days passed. My room was on the third floor and had a lovely view out to a tree-lined boulevard and across to a beautiful park. Although I was given excellent care, with nurses and doctors frequently checking on me, I also had quiet times which were very rewarding. From the beginning, I felt confident that Swami would cancel any cancer which might be present, and each time I spoke to Him about it in my heart, He assured me that it was already taken care of.

Raye visited me daily. He was praying for me continually. He said that his constant prayer was that Baba be with us both, hold our hands, hear our prayers, heal us both in body, mind, and soul, take our hearts, cleanse our thoughts, words, and deeds, and fill us with His grace until we merged in Him. This is still his daily prayer, as printed on page 121.

My dear friends at the ashram kept me supplied with fruit baskets, flower arrangements, books, and love. Without a doubt, this was the most pleasant hospital stay I have ever had. The thing that contributed the most to that pleasantness was the genuine caring of the doctors and nurses. They were lovely, warm, human beings--not just part of the medical machinery. The dear endocrinologist came every day to reassure me in regard to my blood sugar. He explained that what I was experiencing was what has been termed "stress diabetes." Any physical or mental stress can cause the pancreas to secrete too little insulin, thus elevating the blood sugar. He said that as soon as the infection in the leg was cleared up that I would no longer require insulin.

But the leg was not responding to the treatment at all. There was no change. It was red. It was swollen. It was very hot. Massive doses of antibiotics were being administered intravenously; the blood sugar was within the normal range; but the infection raged on. It had now been eight days with no improvement. The doctors were clearly disappointed--maybe even discouraged. So, I intensified my prayers to Swami. I had wanted to put His vibhuti on my leg from the very beginning, but as it seemed impossible to do so without stirring up some disturbance among the doctors and nurses, I had not. Now it seemed to me to be urgent to do that. Baba's vibhuti would surely heal the leg, whether anything else would or not.

One of the requirements during these eight days had been that I keep my leg higher than my head as I lay in the bed. So it was in that extremely uncomfortable position that I began to petition Swami to tell me what to do. I wearied His ears with every promise He has ever made to care for mankind in general and me in particular. Finally, I said, "Swami, I really want to put Your vibhuti on my leg, but it doesn't seem humanly wise to do it here in the hospital. Please, please, just give me a sign, or an answer that I can't mistake. Let me know that it's all right to use the vibhuti, or else tell me that You will take care of me through Your instruments, the doctors. I am listening for Your answer."

A few minutes later I needed to get out of bed for a moment. As I had taken two or three steps, I was suddenly aware of something passing by my face. Almost immediately I heard a small "plop" on the floor. Looking down, I saw a plastic packet filled with vibhuti. I was ecstatic. I crawled back into the bed, opened the packet, and poured the entire contents over the red, angry, feverish, somewhat sticky leg. I carefully smoothed it over the entire leg, from my toes to my hip. There was plenty to cover the whole area.

I then quickly resumed my "leg above the head" position, fully expecting either a doctor or a nurse to appear at any moment. Hardly twenty minutes had passed since I arrived that someone had not come in to check on me and ask to see the leg. Time passed. No one came. My dinner was served. The after-dinner blood check was made, but no one asked to see the leg. My bedtime snack came. I went to sleep and awakened at six o'clock the following morning.

The doctor came bustling into the room, saying, "Let's see the leg." I pulled back the sheet, which I felt sure would be gray with vibhuti, but there was not one grain anywhere. The leg showed no sign at all that anything out of the ordinary had happened. However, the doctor was overjoyed. He said, "Oh, we've finally got it! It's dramatically better." And so it was. I remembered the little piece of enameled artwork which I had brought with me on this trip. It says, "The Lord always listens," and the words are surrounded by pink flowers.

Calamity, danger, and death cannot be avoided for all time; they are inevitable factors of life; you have to learn to live bravely with them. This can be accomplished only by uninterrupted prayer, not by spurts of worship actuated by sudden fear. Purify your hearts, your thoughts, feelings, emotions, speech; strengthen your nobler impulses; then no panic can un-nerve you; nothing can shake your stability, your Prasanthi.

Your prayers will be heard and answered; the Lord has no distinction of big or small, of high or low. (page 137)

When in difficulty, pray for guidance before jumping in any direction. Men will give you advice only as far as their cleverness can reach, but the Lord who illumines dullness into intelligence will reveal to you the way out of the dilemma. Ask the Lord and He will answer. (page 173)

Have patience and wait prayerfully. Prayer can bring about the impossible. Recite the glory of the Lord and repeat in the cavern of your heart His Name. That will bring success. (page 181)

Sathya Sai Baba
Sathya Sai Speaks, Vol. II

Chapter Nineteen

HE TOUCHED ME

With the infection under control, it was now time for the growth to be removed. I was given every consideration which could be imagined. The surgeon told me that he had called in the finest anesthesiologist in Southern India. He assured me that the entire experience would be painless and without unpleasant after effects.

I never doubted him. Knowing that Baba was the only Doer, the Great Physician, and Lord of the Universe, I was firm in my belief that only good was going on. Baba has said, "Welcome blows of fate, misfortune, misery as gold welcomes the crucible, hammer, and anvil, in order to become a jewel." **(Sathya Sai Speaks Vol. III,** Chap. 12)

Each time I thought of the growth, it seemed to me that some dark thought form, which had perhaps been attached to me for many lifetimes, was now going to be cut away--removed by Sai's grace. This was a time for rejoicing.

The operation was a complete success. I came out from under the anesthetic without the slightest distress, and there were no painful after effects. Whatever needed to be removed, had been removed, and all was well.

By this time I was known to many of the nurses, the orderlies, and various members of the hospital staff. On one occasion, I was visited by the executive director of the hospital, who was introduced to me by the endocrinologist. I was never lonely. The young men, in particular, seemed to thoroughly enjoy coming in for a chat. I knew that Baba, as always, was keeping me well-supplied with sons.

Two days after the operation, the biopsy report came back "non-malignant." "Oh, Swami, thank you for canceling the cancer," I said to Him many times. Since I had acknowledged that it was His grace that the growth had been discovered and removed, I certainly must acknowledge that it was also His grace that the growth had not been malignant.

I had missed darshan for two weeks! That was my greatest regret of the entire hospital stay. So, now it was time to go back and do what I had come from the United States to do: have Swami's darshan. I persuaded the doctor to release me a little earlier than he would really have preferred, and went back to the ashram.

My first darshan after my return, Swami didn't come anywhere near me. The second day, He didn't come. The third day passed, and I was still very weak and totally ignored. When four days went by, and Swami didn't appear to even know that I was there, I began to get depressed. I forgot what wonderful grace had been given me, and I felt that He had forsaken and forgotten me completely. Things looked so black that on one occasion I even told Raye that I didn't want to come back to live in India. Raye was steady as a rock. He just replied, "Honey, you'll feel differently soon."

Eight days had now gone by since my return from the hospital. Swami had not even given me a glance. My friends were disturbed that I was so physically weak and so mentally depressed. On the ninth day, after I had given up expecting that He might come where I was, He did. He walked up, stood in front of me, looked deeply into my eyes, and, without saying anything, took my hand and held it tenderly. Of course, it was probably for only a few seconds, but it seemed a marvelously long time. As He touched me, I felt vital energy flow into my hand, up my arm, and throughout my body. When He walked away, I was totally rejuvenated--strong, healthy, and very, very happy.

The transformation was clearly evident to everybody. At least a dozen people commented that I looked like a different person from the one who had come to darshan. Whereas that person was pale, I was a healthy pink. She had had a long face. I was glowing. She had barely made it down the four stairs from the guest house; I climbed back up the same four with renewed energy.

For the next four days, Swami spoke to me or touched me each day. On one occasion, I held out the beautiful topaz earrings with His picture behind the gems, which Raye had had made for me several years ago. I wanted them blessed--imbued with His energy. As He blessed them, He took the fleshy part of my hand at the base of my thumb and tweaked it with His thumb and forefinger. After darshan, several people hastened to tell me that He had pinched me on the Venus love mound, but they couldn't tell me why or what the meaning was. I still don't know exactly, but I'm sure that it was one of His many expressions of Love.

On another occasion, He pinched me in the exact center of my palm. Anybody out there have a theory? If so, write to me at Prasanthi Nilayam. There are as many ways for Swami to express love as there are stars in the heavens or drops of water in the ocean. But my own expressions for right now are more limited. One day when He stopped in front of me and looked into my eyes so sweetly, my heart filled with love until it became impossible not to express it. I said, "Oh, I love you so much, Swami." He replied, "I love you, too, Sir!"

So, here we are again. What does He mean when He addresses a lady as "Sir"? My dictionary says that "Sir" is a respectful term of address used to a man. I'm sure that for one thing it means that Swami recognizes no differences. He loves all the same, without regard for race, religion, social status, financial standing, or gender. And by His respectful address, He also acknowledges that the addressee is God. Whatever reason He has, He can call me "Sir" anytime!

* * * * * * * * *

> *I never do any act which is devoid of significance or speak a word devoid of purpose.*
>
> Sathya Sai Baba
> **Sathya Sai Speaks, Vol. II,** Chap. 37

He Touched Me

Shackled by a heavy burden,
'Neath a load of guilt and shame,
Then the hand of Baba touched me,
And now I am no longer the same.

He touched me, Oh! He touched me.
And, Oh, the joy that floods my soul!
Something happened and now I know,
Sai touched me and made me whole.

Since I met this blessed Savior,
Since He cleansed and made me whole,
I will never cease to love Him.
I'll serve Him while eternity rolls.

He touched me, Oh! He touched me.
And, Oh, the joy that floods my soul!
Something happened and now I know,
Sai touched me and made me whole.

"I love you, too, Sir!"

Chapter Twenty

VERY, VERY HAPPY

But my lessons were not over yet. It so happened that on one evening I became extremely sick at my stomach. I was violently ill, frequently regurgitating, and barely able to lift my head to do so. By morning, I was hardly able to speak.

Raye was beside me every minute, but he asked if I would mind if he went to darshan. I told him to go on since there really was nothing he could do for me. After darshan, however, he came in to tell me that the executive director of the Apollo Hospital, Dr. Krishnaswamy, had been in darshan. Raye had told him how sick I was and he told Raye that he would bring my doctors back from Bangalore as quickly as he could get them.

The surgeon, the endocrinologist, and Dr. Krishnaswamy all came the hour's journey from Bangalore to make sure that I was not suffering from anything related to my operation. Their examination revealed that I had in some way gotten food poisoning. It certainly was not from anything I had eaten from the Western canteen. The food is not only delicious, it is prepared in scrupulously clean surroundings by devotees who volunteer to do the work out of love for Swami. No one had become ill except me, so I must have done something careless, though we were never able to determine what that was.

At any rate, the doctors prescribed medication which eliminated the illness almost as quickly as it had appeared. Although the entire episode had lasted only slightly over twenty-four hours, I felt that I had never before been so sick. The next morning when I went to darshan, I was again extremely weak, pale, and listless. When Baba came to me, He asked, "How are you?" I replied in my most pitiful voice, "Oh, I've been soooo sick, Swami." He smiled, saying, "Very, very happy!"

Although I was startled by His answer, I was also amused. I knew that, as with every word He utters, these words had not been said lightly. They had a message for me. My job was to decode it, learn it, and live out from it. I had agreed that "Whatever happens has to happen." I know that He is the director of the play, and that every line in the script, the dialogue and the stage directions, are for the purpose of freeing us from the delusion and illusion of being a body. But why would He be happy that I had been so sick? I shared His words with several others, and they did not seem to be certain of Swami's meaning either.

It was not until I got back to the States and was browsing through **Sathya Sai Speaks, Vol. VIII** one afternoon that I found Baba's own explanation. It came at the perfect time, since I would be writing this chapter very soon. (I just **think** I'm writing this book. He has been writing it all along.) Whatever He wants to say, He puts it in the forefront of my mind or right in front of my eyes. And so He presented the following answer to the question I was asking:

> *Several devotees come to me and complain, "Lord! I am suffering from*

this problem," "I am suffering from some headache," "I am suffering from stomach ache." I give all of them the same reply, "Santhosham" (I am happy) to everyone. When a bereaved wife tells me that her husband has departed, then also I say "Santhosham."

You may wonder why I give the same reply to all such persons. Santhosham is not the common type of joy or happiness. It is not the transient, trivial pleasure you get from worldly success or material gain. "San" means anything gained through fair means, honorable methods. "Thosham" is sacred, holy exaltation, ecstasy.

Of all the gifts you receive from God, the greatest gift is Santhosham. The opposite of Santhosham is sorrow, which is the fruit of Asha or desire that arouses hope and almost always results in disappointment or despair. One Asha engenders another; one desire proliferates into a hundred, even when it is fulfilled.

Asha or desire is like the shadow caused by the morning sun—it gets longer when you run to catch it. It tantalizes you and makes you a fool. It knows no justification and has no end. So, Santhosham is the supreme blessing of the Lord, who in His Infinite Love, puts an end to that unquenchable thirst. No wealth or other attainment can equal it in efficacy. Santhosham is the culmination of desire in full contentment and sacred satiety.

Sathya Sai Baba
Sathya Sai Speaks, Vol. VIII, *Ch. 25*

Chapter Twenty-One

THE SWEETNESS OF SWAMI

Dr. P. R. Krishnaswamy and his wife, Rukmini, quickly became treasured friends. The doctor would stop by our room after darshan to check on me, and Rukmini would accompany him. The four of us had many wonderful conversations, Swami, of course, being the subject.

As we shared our backgrounds, how we came to know about Sai Baba, and other experiences along our spiritual path, we learned that Rukmini had attended a Christian school and college, combining her spiritual education with selfless service. She felt very close to Jesus but seemed to have no need for any church or organization. Her lifelong prayer has been to be like Jesus, healing and helping others.

Dr. Krishnaswamy said that he had always felt great admiration for Mahatma Gandhi and that Gandhi's inspiration was Jesus, too. It was on the basis of Jesus' teachings that Gandhi took his firm stand for nonviolence. However, the doctor found that his study of the physical sciences caused him to drift away from any tendency he might have had toward religion. On February 26, 1991, he read a quotation in regard to Sai Baba's hospital in Puttaparthi. It spoke of compassion for the poor and the fact that medical services were provided without charge. Dr. Krishnaswamy said that it sounded very much like the mission of Christ.

Rukmini said that twenty-five years ago she had visited Baba's ashram in Bombay and had eaten dinner there with Him. That night she dreamed that she saw Swami in a blue car in a parking lot. She said, "He looked at me sternly, but with love." Hardly a day passed, she said, that she did not recall the dream. However, she always felt that her life was being fulfilled through her service activities, so she never made an effort to see Bhagavan again. Her dear friend in Bombay spoke to her of Baba many times, but Rukmini never felt the need to find out anything more for herself.

It was on June 19, 1991, at 3:00 a.m., that Dr. Krishnaswamy dreamed of sitting in a space car at an airport and of his friend, who was a Baba devotee, standing on the tarmac nearby. He heard Swami's voice say, "Take him with you. He's stranded here." He obediently took the friend inside the space car.

The doctor was not at all interested in Sathya Sai Baba because, as he said, "Miracles turned me off." But the dream was so vivid that he told Rukmini about it as soon as they were both awake that morning. Then, at 7:20 a.m., a call came from the Vice-Chancellor of the Sathya Sai University, saying that Sai Baba would like to meet with the doctor on the following Sunday. Dr. Krishnaswamy agreed to be at darshan on that day.

When he attempted to persuade Rukmini to go with him, however, he met with some resistance. Rukmini takes a leading role in working for the help and healing of severely handicapped children. An extremely important meeting had been scheduled for that Sunday morning, and so Rukmini told her husband that she could not possibly go with him to darshan. She continued to insist that she could not go until the very last minute. But suddenly she agreed that someone else could handle the meeting and got into the car with the doctor.

When they were both seated in darshan, Swami came out. He went to Dr. Krishnaswamy and told him to go inside. In order that there be no misunderstanding, the doctor said, pointing to the ladies' side, "My wife is over there." Swami asked, "What happened to her meeting?" Then He went to the ladies' side, telling Rukmini to go inside. When they entered the interview room, Swami Himself brought in a chair for Rukmini. She said that she knew then that Sai Baba was totally without ego, and added, "From that day, I have never wavered in my devotion to Him."

During that first interview, Swami invited the doctor to visit Puttaparthi and to take a tour of the Super Specialty Hospital. He was very happy to accept the invitation. In an interview on November 14, 1991, Swami manifested a gold ring with a green stone for him--the green symbolizing healing. As they went out onto the veranda, Swami told those seated there, "He is going to help Me in the hospital."

Dr. Krishnaswamy said, "That was the first I knew of it!" But he has been willing and eager to follow Swami's instructions. He will leave the Apollo Hospital in October, 1994, and spend a year in Bombay at an excellent hospital there, then report to Swami "to help Him in the hospital." Rukmini's plans are to continue her work with the severely handicapped children.

Raye and I were delighted to be invited to their home for lunch one day. Raye was fascinated with Rukmini's stories of her work--even feeling a strong desire to join her in it. We had a delightful meal and stimulating, inspiring conversation. Then, the highlight of the day was a visit to their puja room. To our surprise, we saw a picture of Jesus in the center of their altar and the picture was dripping with amrit.

Rukmini said that she had admired the picture one day in the home of one of her friends. She especially liked it because it was Jesus as the good shepherd, lovingly tending his flock. She always thought of him in that way--serving all who came. Her friend said that she had enjoyed the picture for several years and that now she would like to give it to Rukmini as an Easter gift.

The picture was in sepia tones. Rukmini had it carefully framed and placed it on the altar in their home. Within a short time, the doctor noticed a sweet smell coming from the picture. Then it began to ooze a slightly sticky substance. The cleaning woman washed it carefully, but the sweet fluid reappeared almost immediately. Finally, they realized that they were being blessed with the manifestation of amrit, and they placed a bowl under the picture to collect the sacred sweetness.

Slowly the picture began to take on color. When I saw the altar for the first time, I was struck by the bright green of the grass. From the original sepia, it is now in full color. Originally the picture itself was printed on very thin paper. As the amrit continued to flow from it, over time the cardboard backing which had been placed behind the picture deteriorated and fell apart, but the picture itself has become thicker and stronger.

As many of Rukmini's friends are Christian, they found this phenomenon of great interest. On one occasion, Rukmini allowed a priest and seven nuns to take the picture from its frame and examine it thoroughly. They could find nothing which explained the continual flow of amrit.

As for myself, it had only been two or three days since I had made the statement that I had never seen any manifestation as it actually appeared. It had been brought to my attention that near Brindavan there were some people who were selling amrit and vibhuti which they claimed had manifested on Baba's pictures in their home. At that time, I sent a prayer Swami's way that someday I might have the privilege of seeing the genuine process of His manifesting amrit or vibhuti without Himself being physically present. I have seen both amrit and vibhuti on His pictures or other holy objects on several occasions, but it has always been inactive during my observation. Now, here I was seeing the amrit as it appeared, manifested by the Will of our Beloved Lord. Once again, Swami answered my prayer in a way that I could never have foreseen.

* * * * * * * * *

In Mysore State there are some who distribute amrit, vibhuti, and other articles, announcing that they are showering from my pictures at their places. They do this free for some weeks, but later they start begging for money, like any common mendicant! This is sin, to ask so, and also to give so. Devotees should keep far away from such places and such persons.

Visualize God in your heart. Why go to such a place or anywhere outside of yourself to see Him? In some other places they announce that I make myself present and communicate through writings on rangoli powder, etc.! I do not do such things! If I come at all to any place, I come directly so that you see me. I do not speak or answer through another person or another medium! Repeat the Name, do Japa, and sing bhajans in your own home; there is no special call for you to come to this place or that. Wherever you are, whatever Name you like, whatever Form pleases you, I bless you if your heart is pure. Avoid pomp, exhibition, boasting; be simple, sincere, and sweet.

Sathya Sai Baba
Sathya Sai Speaks, Vol. VIII, Chap. 6

Bhakti is something sweet, soothing, refreshing, and restoring. It must confer patience and fortitude. The Bhakta will not be perturbed if another gets an interview first or if another is given greater consideration. He is humble and bides his time. He knows that there is a higher power that knows more and that it is just and impartial. In the light of that knowledge, the Bhakta will communicate his troubles and problems only to his Lord. He will not humiliate himself by talking about them to all and sundry, for what can a man who is as helpless as himself do to relieve him?

It is only those who have that implicit faith in God, who communicate only with the Lord and none else, who deserve amrit. The Sthuladeha should be ever immersed in satsang; the thoughts and feelings should be ever immersed in the contemplation of the Glory of the Lord. That is the sign of the true devotee.

He who shouts and swears and advertises his worries to everyone he meets, craving for sympathy, can never be a true devotee, a Bhakta. Such men are miscalled devotees. They make earnest men lose faith in Godly ways; earnest men feel that they are superior to these pseudo-Bhaktas. And this is a fact.

It is a great responsibility to tread the Godward path. There is no backsliding, no stopping half-way, no tardy pace, no side lane on such a pilgrimage. It is up, up, and always up, right to the crest of the mountain.

Though your responsibility may be greater than others, take it from me, you are luckier than they. Do not deny with the tongue what you have relished in the heart. Do not bear false witness to your own truly felt experience. Do not carp and talk cynically of the very thing you have revered and adored when the company into which you fall begins to banter and jest in their disbelief.

It is said that the Bhakta can find the Lord everywhere easily but that the Lord cannot find a Bhakta so easily. Yes, it is difficult to find a Bhakta who has that unshaken faith, that attitude of complete self-surrender. Such an attitude can come only by repeating the Name, constantly, sincerely, and continuously—as continuously as the act of breathing—feeling it to be equally essential for life. That is the recitation, the spiritual exercise, and the meditation for you all. Repeating the name like this will immerse you forever in amrit, not just put a drop on your tongue.

Sathya Sai Baba
Sathya Sai Speaks, Vol. II, Chap. 3

Let His Will be done—this should be your guideline. The Emperor of the Cholas sought to visit the Srirangam Gopuram Temple, of which he had heard much. He got his chariot ready to go and started forward many times over a six-month period, but each time a recluse in ochre robes with a rosary around his neck and a halo around his head intercepted the vehicle. When the emperor alighted to honor him, he kept him engaged in such enchanting conversation that he forgot about his journey and its goal.

One day when he was lamenting over his failure to fill his eyes with the glory of Srirangam, the Lord appeared before him and said, "Why do you lament? I am the Master who came to you whenever you tried to set out for Srirangam. Recognize Me in all; that is the genuine pilgrimage to Srirangam." Consider all whom you meet as the Lord of Srirangam, your Master. Show untarnished love towards all who come to you.

What is the service that the ocean with all its mass of waters does? It cannot slake the thirst of a single human being. What is the profit if a miser lives a hundred years? This is my message to you this day: do not exhibit anger, grief, or pain. Be happy; spread happiness around you. Sweetness alone is the offering that God likes.

Sathya Sai Baba
Sathya Sai Speaks, Vol. V, Chap. 58

Chapter Twenty-Two

MORE SWEETNESS

Speaking to the devotees one afternoon in Brindavan, Swami spoke of the importance of being sweet. He said that each of us should always speak sweetly as well as behave sweetly toward others. It was a wonderful discourse and I looked forward to obtaining a tape recording of it in order to print it here. To my regret, it seemed not to have been taped, and I was never able to obtain a record of His beautiful words.

After returning to Cherry Valley, I was still unable to accept the fact that I could not get anything that Swami had said recently about sweetness. It seemed to me to be essential in order to get across the full message of this book: **Life Is Love, Enjoy It!** After finishing Chapter Twenty-One, I sat down, closed my eyes, and began to speak to Swami about the missing discourse. I asked Him to please help me provide the material that he wished readers of this book to have to complete the teachings which have just been presented.

I put out my hand to the bookshelf beside me, picked up the January 1994 issue of **Sanathana Sarathi**, opened it to page 1, and began reading Swami's Christmas '93 discourse, entitled "Let Love Prevail." To my amazement it covered everything I had hoped for and more. So, here in Swami's own words, you can read everything I have been attempting to share with you on the preceding and following pages. He began, as He so often does, with a little song.

Whom the Mohammedans adore as Allah,
The Christians as Jehovah,
The Vaishnavites as the Lotus-eyed Lord,
The Saivites as Sambhu,
That God who confers on all
Long life, health, and prosperity,
Is One Only. Have this conviction.
The Lord is all Love;
Love is His Divine Form;
That Love is the redeeming mantra
For all beings in this world.
Without experiencing a fragment of that Love,
How can you experience the Divine, Oh, man?

EMBODIMENTS OF DIVINE LOVE!

If one object has to combine with another, or one individual has to associate with another, love is the basis for the affinity. The entire world is filled with love. The world is Love and Love is the world.

In every human being, love is present as an effulgence which shines in his feelings. Love is life, and life is Love. Even as the power to burn is natural for fire, and the power to cool is natural for water, love is a natural trait for man. Without it, he ceases to be human.

LOVE AND LIFE

Love is an inborn quality in man. It is his life-breath. We nourish a sapling with great love.

When the sapling grows and later becomes a dry plant, we cast it away without any concern. How much love did we lavish on the sapling? We cherished it as long as it had life. After it became dry and lifeless, we had no love for it. From infancy we bear love for the mother who has borne us and reared us. But when she passes away, the dead body is burned without any attachment. What is it that was loved earlier? The living being was loved. Hence life and love are mutually inter-related.

Men today tend to forget the love-life relationship. Love today is mingled with self-interest. In the tree of every man's life, there is the fruit of love. To enjoy this fruit, the rind that covers it has to be removed at the outset. The seeds in the fruit also have to be removed. The sweet juice in the fruit can be enjoyed only after the rind and the seeds have been removed. In the fruit of the tree of life, the rind is egoism (ahamkara). The seeds in that fruit are the selfish interests of man. Only when the ego and selfishness are eliminated, can the sweet juice of love be experienced. The **Upanishads** *describe this love as "the sweet juice that is nectarine (amrit) and the Supreme (Brahman)." This means that the juice of love is nectar itself, is verily the Divine (Brahman). It is life itself. It is the Divine Effulgence.*

This juice of love is equal to Brahman. It confers immortality on man and fills him with Divine bliss. Men today are unable to grasp the meaning of this Love Principle. It is essentially Divine in its nature. Hence, "Love is God; live in Love."

Most people, however, in their fascination for sensuous pleasures and worldly objects, are deem-

ing the attachments to these as love. Immersed in selfish pursuits and interests, men seek everything for only selfish reasons and have no regard for the transcendental. Everything is desired for self-enjoyment and not out of love for the sake of love. We should love for the sake of the Divine, to realize the eternal. Love should be for experiencing the effulgence of wisdom (jnana).

THE MARTYRDOM OF JESUS

Love is thus an amalgam of sweetness, effulgence, and wisdom. Compassion is the reflection of love. Jesus is the embodiment of compassion. He looked with compassion on the poor and the miserable and gave them succor. In those days, people used to treat birds and animals without pity in the temple in Jerusalem. Jesus sought to put an end to those cruel practices.

From those times to the present, those who care for the well-being of all living beings and humanity have been subjected to many trials and tribulations. Good people are always pursued by difficulties and troubles. The messiahs, the prophets, saints, and God-men have always suffered from troubles and ordeals of various kinds. You should not feel bothered about the ordeals which you pass through. Have faith in God. When you live up to the truths you believe in, you will be indifferent to what others think.

Jesus was unaffected by the persecution to which he was subjected on a charge of treason. Moreover, whatever attempts may be made to suppress good people, their goodness cannot be extinguished.

A fine diamond, even if it is in a heap of garbage,
Will not lose its brilliance or its value.
A pumpkin, even if it is grown beside a hedge,
Will not lose its sweetness.
A peahen's egg, even if it is hatched in a crow's nest,
Will not lose its colors.

Likewise, the glory and greatness of good men will suffer no diminution in whatever circumstances or situation they may be placed. Such Divine effulgence is shining in every human being. Love is an expression of this effulgence. To manifest this love, men must be prepared to bear every kind of suffering.

Can the sweet juice of the sugarcane
Be had for making sugar
Without the cane being crushed?

The human body is like the sugarcane, filled with the juice of love. It is only when the body is subjected to hardship that the divine, sweet juice of love can flow from it. Without trouble to the body, pains to the mind, and control of the feelings, how can you expect to experience the Divine? Men today aspire for liberation with no suffering on their part. God's love is not to be secured so easily. The precious gem of love can be obtained only in the bazaar of sacrifice. It is valued only in the Kingdom of Love, so how can it be purchased in a market of cheap wares?

DEVOTION AND SELFISHNESS

Man's devotion these days is suffused with selfishness. Everything he does stems from self-interest. The first requisite is the giving up of selfishness. There must be a curb on egoistic conceit and possessiveness. The mind must be submerged in pure love.

You may have heard about the life of St. Paul. In the beginning he was bitterly opposed to Jesus. One day Jesus appeared in his dream and said: "Saul, are you not a human being? Is it proper for you to revile one who has done you no harm, has entertained no evil thoughts about you, and has not led you into wrong ways? What harm have I done to you? Why are you abusing me? This is sheer folly. You are thereby demeaning yourself. Beware! Beware!" After uttering this warning, Jesus vanished. On waking up in the morning, Saul (as Paul was known before his transformation) lamented that he had been false to his human nature by deriding and condemning his fellow beings. He felt that Jesus was doing many good deeds. He was one who could not bear the sight of others' sufferings. He was showering love on every one. Saul felt that it was a sin to revile such a person. From that date, Saul became a devotee of Jesus and came to be known at St. Paul. (This story is related in the King James Version of the **Bible** in the book of Acts, Chapter 9.)

In spite of all the love and blessings they receive and the benefits they derive from the Avatars, some devotees turn against the Divine when their selfish desires are not fulfilled.

TRADUCERS OF GOD

There are three types of traducers of God. In the first category are those who have no belief in God and always indulge in abuse of God. Without faith, how can there be any devotion? And without devotion, how can there be love? Without love, how can anyone be termed human? The words of such a person are worthless.

The second category of persons are those who adore God when their desires are fulfilled and deride God when their wishes are not satisfied. They imagine that they have a right to receive favors from God. Such petty-minded persons revile God. Their desires are sky-high, but their efforts are minimal. Their spiritual efforts are insignificant. Nevertheless, they criticize God when their insatiable desires are not satisfied.

The third category of persons are those who turn against God out of jealousy. They cannot bear the prosperity or position of others (towards whom, they think, God is partial). There is a remedy for almost every malady, but none at all for the disease of jealousy. The envious indulge in calumny against God.

It is because of the ubiquitous presence of these three categories of anti-God men that spirituality and the divine feeling of love have become rare commodities today.

ONENESS WITH GOD

There is a Vedic saying: "The knower of Brahman becomes Brahman himself." You are aware of the Godly man, Moses, described in the Bible.

He was one who was ceaselessly praying to the Lord. He was a fervent lover of God. His intense devotion and love ultimately transformed his face and filled it with a divine radiance.
(See Exodus, Chapter 34, in the King James Version of the Bible.)

Likewise, the Gopikas, through their intense devotion to Krishna, became the living image of Krishna. Ratnakara, who was a highwayman in his early years, acquired the radiance of Rama by continually chanting the name of Rama.

Whatever God you worship, adore him with a sense of Oneness. Bodies may be two, but the heart is one. This is the feeling with which God should be worshiped. Only then can you reach the state when you can declare: "You and I are One."

THE BITTER BECOMES SWEET

How this state is to be realized is illustrated by a biblical episode. Once St. John saw an angel holding a little book. He asked what the little book was and was told that it was the doctrine of love. He asked for the book and the angel gave it to him, saying: "You must eat this book. When you are consuming it, its taste will be bitter. But after you have completely digested it, it will become very sweet." "Eating the book" means absorbing the contents of the book and practicing its teachings.

The experience while digesting the book was bitter as had been declared by the angel. However, in due course, there was a great transformation in St. John. His speech acquired a unique sweet-

ness. His looks were sweet. Everything about him became sweet. What does this mean? It signifies the truth that you should completely identify yourself with Divine Love, which you now seek from God. This love is not a purchasable commodity.

Today devotion is treated as an exercise in shareholding, a kind of business partnership. But this is not right. The devotees should feel "Everything is Thine." It is only when there is such a feeling of total surrender that the nature of Divine Love can be comprehended.

MESSENGERS OF SATHYA SAI

There is nothing in the world easier than the spiritual path. It has to be followed in the form of loving service. To demonstrate to the world the beauty, the sweetness, and the glory of selfless and loving service, the association called "Messengers of Sathya Sai" was formed from among the old students of the Sathya Sai College for Women at Anantapur. These girls, regardless of the families into which they married and the countries where they went to live, pledged themselves to carry on their service activities. What this vow means should be properly understood. Men have greater freedom to act as they please. Married women have less freedom. They come under the unfluence of their husbands and in-laws. Despite these constraints, these former students have not only carried on their service activities but have also interested their husbands in service....

The annual report of the Messengers of Sathya Sai mentions that their members are rendering service in different countries like Kuwait, Australia, and New Zealand. Their varied service activities are highly commendable. I am confident that very soon their activities will cover the entire world and promote the welfare of every country....

LOVING SERVICE AND SACRIFICE

Service should be your watchword. The spirit of sacrifice is essential. To speak about devotion without a spirit of sacrifice is meaningless.

Many of the women carry on their service activities in spite of the troubles which they face from their husbands. This shows their spirit of sacrifice. The Messengers of Sathya Sai are doing signal service. They need not confine themselves to their own members. They should try to draw other women into service activities and strive to improve the living conditions of the poor.

FOLLOW SAI'S TEACHINGS

If the name of Jesus is glorified all over the world today, it is because of His boundless love. He served the lowly and the lost and, in the end, offered his life itself as a sacrifice. How many of those who call themselves devotees of Jesus are following His teachings? Those who claim to worship Rama, how far are they following His example? How many professed devotees of Krishna are living up to His teachings? There are many who claim to be Sai devotees. How many of them are following the message of Sai? If everyone seeks the answer within himself, he may see that it is a zero. Anyone who claims to be a Sai devotee should dedicate his life to Sai ideals. That is true devotion and real penance. That is the hallmark of humanness. It will be reflected in love, which will find expression in compassion, and which will generate true bliss.

MAKE LOVE THE BREATH OF YOUR LIFE

The greatest quality in every man is love. When love is absent, evil qualities like hatred and jealousy rear their heads. Make love the breath of your life.

Sathya Sai Baba
From Discourse of December 25, 1993
As reported in **Sanathana Sarathi,** January 1994

Chapter Twenty-Three

WEARING THE OCHRE ROBE

When Crystal and Brian Pearl had left Kodaikanal without having been able to have an interview with Swami or obtain a robe for the Sai Baba Center which meets in their home, I had agreed to ask Swami again for them if I got the chance. I had asked Him twice now, and each time He had replied, "I will give." As the time grew nearer for us to return to the States and the robe was still not in our hands, I pondered Swami's answer at some length.

I recalled the incident in which Swami had looked at the little medallion I was wearing, telling me that He would make me a good one. Later, on the advice of one of Swami's longtime devotees, I myself had a "good one" made by a jeweler, and Swami has blessed it many times. The lesson here was that the "I" is One and that One is All. We can read these words, we can listen intently when Swami speaks them, but to truly realize their truth and live our lives based on that understanding requires faith and steady practice. Swami puts it this way:

> *...Who am I? I is the most frequently used word; it recurs many times a second in conversation. I said, I saw, I went, I heard, I have this, I am king, I am a ryot, I am a child, I am a pundit, I am tall, I am lean—but who is this I that has these attributes and possessions? The* ***Upanishads*** *declare that the I is not the personalized individual;*

that is a delusion. It is not limited to the body which it inhabits. It is the most universal of categories, it is the eternal absolute, the Paramatma. It is the omnipresent universal consciousness, the Sat-Chit-Ananda (Being-Awareness-Bliss).

How can this Truth be known as an indelible authentic experience? That is the key to liberation, to eternal joy, to the conquest of grief. The trouble is that man is shaped into a basically incompetent individual by the activities of many lives; he is born with inherited twists and turns.... Only faith and steady practice can overcome this handicap.

Man is burdened with the delusion that the true is the false, that the temporary is eternal. Long identification has trained him so; so, he has to be re-educated into the right vision. The truest thing, the fact that persists unchanged, is this I itself. All else is unreal, appearing as real. You may ask, 'How can this I be true? I grow, I am healthy once, I fall ill, I grow old.' But, in and through all the growth and decay, the I persists. 'I slept nicely,' you say after a sleep experience during which you were not aware of the body, the senses, or even the mind—not to speak of the external world.

There are three desires from which no 'I' can escape. 'I must live' is the first. The will to live is overpowering and paramount. This is the urge for immortality. The desire to know is the second. This, too, is an unquenchable thirst and is an indication of the omniscience of which the I is the inheritor. The desire for joy is the third, prompting man behind the senses into the outer world for pleasures. This evidence shows that deep in the core of the I there is a spring of Ananda which seeks its mate and its fulfilment. When we speak of the yard of cloth, the liter of honey, the foot or yard, these are first fixed and then the measure or length is determined in terms of the already determined standard, isn't it? So, too, the I is Sat (Immortal Existence), Chit (Universal Knowledge), and Ananda (Absolute Bliss). Individuals are measured and weighed according to the approximation of each to the standard of the universal I.

Sathya Sai Baba
Sathya Sai Speaks, Vol. VII, Chap. 53

In the light of this instruction from Swami, I pondered many times His saying "I will give." Was it my place to take some action, or was patience the virtue which was required? This question was uppermost in my mind one day when a friend came to my room. She mentioned to me that she was having a robe made by Swami's tailor in the hope that Baba would bless it for use by a Center in her country. The incident seemed a clear directive to me to do the same. Praying again that Swami not allow me to do anything contrary to His will, I sent a message to the tailor that I would like to see him. While waiting for him to appear, I pondered Swami's words again.

> *The I in you is Paramatma Himself. The I is the tiny waveling that plays with the wind for a moment over the deep waters of the sea. The wave gives you the impression that it is separate from the timeless, azure ocean below, but it is just an appearance—a creation of the two ideas, Name and Form. Get rid of the two ideas, and the wave disappears into the sea; its reality flashes upon you and you know. Paramatma reveals Its Glory as Love in man.*
>
> Sathya Sai Baba
> **Sathya Sai Speaks**, Vol. II, Chap. 2

Was the action I was considering taking a loving one? Would it be a blessing to others? As it seemed to me that the answer to both these questions was "yes," I finally completely surrendered all of the ego-doubts and awaited the arrival of the tailor. When he came, I told him that I would like to order two robes. Since the robe being used by the Cherry Valley Center was one which Swami had given me and I would wish to take it with me, it seemed only proper that I should replace it with another.

The tailor was willing to make the two robes exactly as he tailored Swami's personal robes. He told me that he would be going to Bombay to pick up some very special material which had been especially manufactured for the purpose of making robes for Swami and that the two new robes would be made from that material.

The tailor was as good as his word. He brought the two beautifully tailored robes in lovely shades of yellow-red (ochre), one having more red pigment than the other. They were incredibly soft, and I felt that I would certainly feel no reluctance to present them to Swami for His blessing because of their quality.

The next morning, feeling completely happy with all that had gone into the obtaining of the robes, I placed them on a silver tray and surrounded them with red roses. As I arrived at the first gate to enter darshan, I was chagrined to hear the head Seva Dal tell the friend who was pushing my wheelchair, "Take her all the way to the back." I gulped and said faintly, "But I've brought robes for Swami to bless." The reply was, "That's all right. You can bring them again tomorrow. Today you go all the way to the back."

Thus it was that I was sitting as far back as the wheelchair could go. The aisle had been filled almost up to the last gate, so I was placed on the bench at that point. Rarely, indeed, did Swami ever come that far back, but there was always tomorrow, as the dear lady had said.

So, when Swami came for darshan, He walked down the aisle on the ladies' side as far as the second gate, then walked across to the men's side. I was enjoying watching the sweet attention that He was giving the men without a thought that He might possibly come back to the ladies' side. However, as He walked toward the center aisle, taking letters from the men and occasionally stopping to speak to some fortunate gentleman, He suddenly looked up, and I felt that He looked directly at me. From that moment, He walked straight across to the ladies' side and came where I was.

I held the robes up to Him, and He gently placed His hand on them, rubbing the material, taking it between His fingers, and patting both robes in blessing. Then He looked into my eyes and asked, "Will you wear these yourself?" I thought surely my ears were playing tricks on me. I did not dare answer. He asked again, "Are you going to wear these yourself?" Again, I refused to believe that He was saying what He said. So He repeated the question for the third time, "You're going to wear these yourself?" I replied, "Oh, Swami, they're for two of Your Centers in the United States." Then He said, "Very good, very happy," and walked on.

I echoed His words, "Very happy," because I was extremely grateful to be able to return to the States with the two robes which He had so lovingly blessed. But He had certainly given me another of His sayings to ponder. What did He mean? Obviously, the question did not refer to my human body fitting into those material robes. That would never happen. And so it was, as most of Swami's questions are, very mundane if looked at from a human standpoint, but deeply significant if deciphered with spiritual understanding.

"Are you going to wear these yourself?

It did, of course, relate to the understanding of "I," which had been the focal point of my study for the weeks preceding the presentation of the robes to Swami for His blessing. The thought that I might ever wear the ochre robe had been the farthest thing from my mind. But, again, if I stop thinking of myself as a wavelet which is different from and separate from the ocean, and begin realizing that the wavelet is **not** different or separate from the ocean but is, in fact, the ocean itself, then maybe I could begin to accept the fact that I might be as worthy to wear the ochre robe as others who do.

But the ochre robe signifies to everyone that the wearer has renounced his attachment to all of the pleasures of the world and that his sole purpose is to help others achieve a higher level of spiritual understanding. Is Swami giving me a hint as to what I should be working toward? He told a story which might be helpful to me in this regard:

> *Detachment, Faith, and Love—these are the pillars on which peace rests. Of these, Faith is crucial. For without it, Sadhana (spiritual practice) is an empty rite. Detachment alone can make Sadhana effective and Love leads quickly to God. Faith feeds the agony of separation from God; detachment canalizes it along the path of God; Love lights the way. God will grant you what you need and deserve; there is no need to ask, no reason to grumble. Be content, be grateful for whatever happens, whenever it happens. Nothing can happen against His Will.*

I am reminded of Karna. In his last moments, he asked from the Lord just one boon. "I do not mind if you condemn me to be born and to face death in an endless cycle; only bless me that in all my many lives I am not constrained to stand before another, with my hand extended, pleading 'give,' and bless me also that in all my lives I am not constrained to send away a supplicant with the word, 'no,' Let not these two words, 'give' and 'no,' emerge from my mouth." A person fixed in detachment and self-control will never ask "give" and can never hear the reply "no," for he is ever content, ever full.

Vivekananda was once asked by a cynical critic why he paraded his renunciation through wearing the ochre robe. He replied, "This is no parade; this is a protection. I am wearing this ochre because, seeing this, no one will approach me for alms or monetary help. I also wear it in order that the word 'no,' which I am averse to pronounce, need not be spoken by me. At the sight of this robe, only seekers of salvation will come near me; for them I have enough to give. I am moved when distressed people come near and I have no money to give them. This dress helps me escape such painful situations." You should so regulate your life that the two words "give" and "no" are not used by you while you live.

Do not grieve, nor be the cause of grief. The very embodiment of Ananda (God) is in you, as in others, as in all else. In spite of a multiplicity of containers, the contained is the same. This is the principle of Sat-Chit-Ananda (Being-Awareness-Bliss). The minutest atom, the mightiest star, both are basically One. All are, in Truth, Brahmam, Divine.... Seen as body, all are distinct; seen as the embodied, Brahmam, all are One.

Sathya Sai Baba
Sathya Sai Speaks, Vol. VII, Chap. 7

So, now I believe that I know the instruction which Swami was giving me when He asked, "Will you wear these yourself?" At least until I receive further enlightenment, I will strive never to ask another to give to me, but to always have faith that Baba is supplying all of my needs. I will also work diligently on never denying another what he asks from me. Between the blessing of the robes and this writing, I have failed to live up to this standard on more than one occasion. However, I will continue my efforts. With Swami's grace, maybe someday I will reach the goal of total detachment, complete faith, and perfect love. That is my prayer.

You may ask me, "How is it possible for a man to be wicked or vicious when his body is the temple of God? His words may be harsh, his actions may be reprehensible, his behavior may be revolting, but he is, nevertheless, Divine! For, look upon him not as a body with a name and form, or a mind with emotions and feelings, or reason with resolutions and conclusions, but as the Atman, the Universal I reflected in the particular i. That i is as pure, peaceful, and expansive as the I of which it is but a wave! Cultivate this attitude of observing everyone, then you can rid your mind of prejudices. The i in him and the i in you are identical, for both derive existence, knowledge, and bliss from the same Absolute I, the Paramatman. If your devotion does not stand by you when you seek to revere the reflections of God in the body-mirrors that move around you, how can you claim to be devoted to God, the Original of which these are but faint and faltering echos? This is the Sadhana I prescribe for you.

Without steady faith and sincere practice of this Sadhana, if you simply come together in groups, preparing and sharing food on every conceivable occasion—even if you sing and extol God—I must say that your efforts are all in vain! Expand your hearts; enlarge your vision; enlarge your circle of kinship; take more and more of your fellow beings into the tabernacle of your heart, adoring them in loving worship. Wisdom is only compassion at its highest; for it is through sympathy that you enter the heart of another and understand him through and through. You go behind the veil of pretense and punditry, convention and custom; you go behind good manners and the fashions that people put on to hide their agony and ignorance from the rest of the world. Finding the unity in this diversity of roles is true wisdom.

Sathya Sai Baba
Sathya Sai Speaks, Vol. VII, Chap. 79

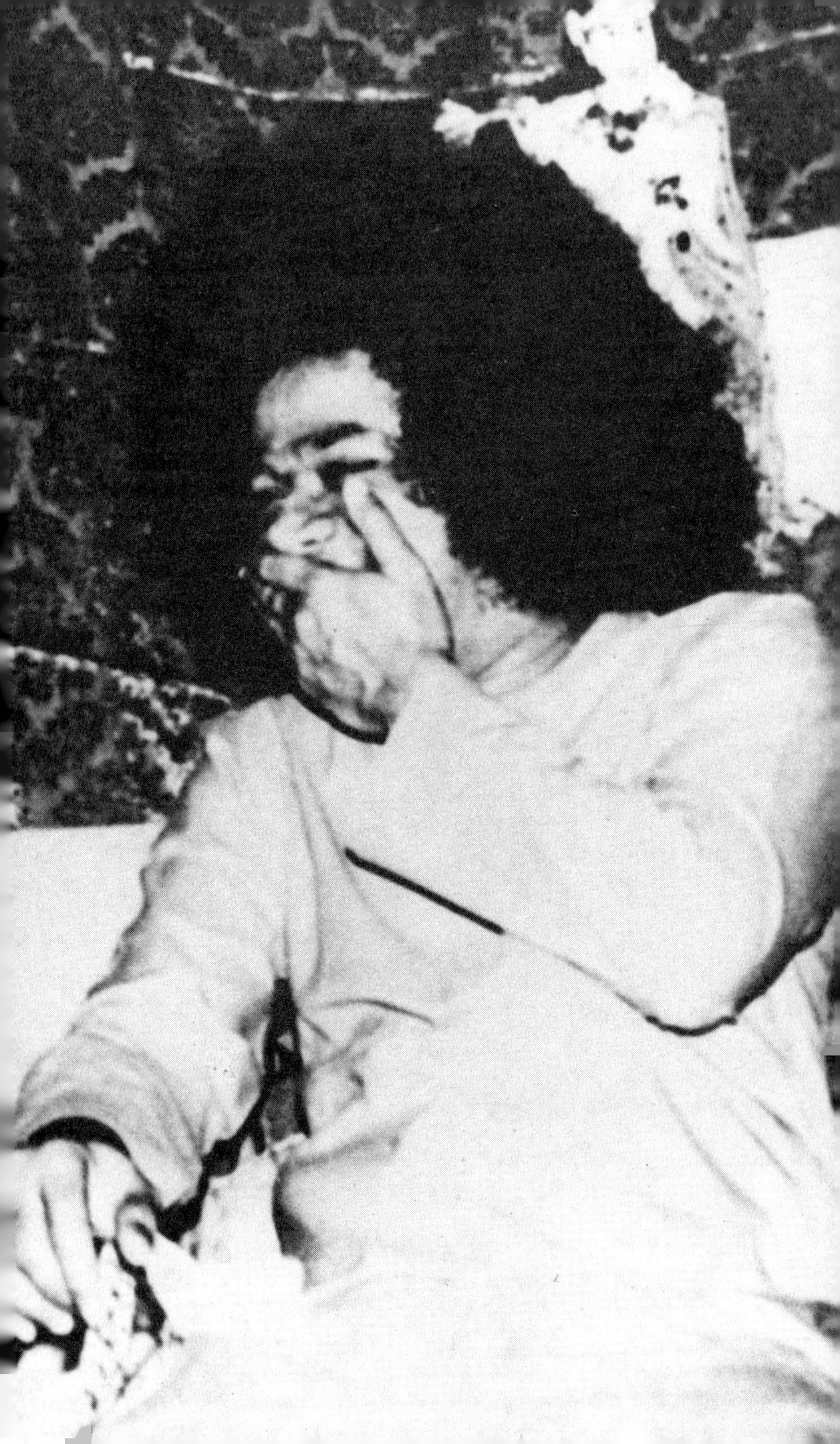

Chapter Twenty-Four

AMAZING GRACE

Before leaving the United States, we had been asked by the Center membership to try to give Swami a donation for the Sathya Sai Books and Publications Trust. We are all so very grateful for the excellent quality and very low prices of the books supplied for devotees by the Trust, that this seemed an appropriate place to put the monies which accumulate in the Center account due to the generosity of members and friends. However, my first attempt to make the donation had resulted in the return of the check. I was told that Swami said that there was no need for the money and that we could probably use it.

Feeling that I had not done an adequate job of explaining why the members wished to donate the money to the Book Trust, I had written a letter explaining our deep desire to make this contribution, why we wanted to do so, and had the letter with me when I went to darshan on July 17, the day before we planned to leave.

It was also uppermost in my thought to ask Swami's permission to leave on July 18, since the rumor had been going around that He had told one group not to travel on July 16, 17, or 18. Although I have long since learned to put little faith in hearsay about what Swami says, I still felt it would not be out of order to ask His permission to leave. Many people do this routinely anyway.

So it was, that on July 17, I arrived at darshan, being pushed by my faithful friend and volunteer, who was told again, "Take her all the way to the back." I think I mumbled something like, "I'm leaving tomorrow," but went along as directed to the rear of the area. This time, the seat which was available as far back as the wheelchair could go was the end one by the last gate. I clutched the letter I had written to Swami, begging Him to accept our contribution to the Trust, and sent up a little prayer that He would give us permission to leave the following day.

As there was a Bal Vikas Conference starting in a day or so, the crowds were growing in size every day. On this morning, devotees were seated all along the roadway outside, under a temporary shelter which had been built between the marriage hall and the university building, all the way back to the last gate. When Swami came out through the gate of the compound, He walked along the roadway, speaking to and accepting letters from those seated outside the covered darshan area. When He finally turned to come inside, He was at the last gate.

I sat holding out the letter, and He came to me. "When are you leaving?" He asked while taking the letter. I replied, "Tomorrow, Swami!" He said, "Go." My reaction was one of great relief. I thought, "Oh, good, He has said that it's all right for us to go tomorrow." As He walked on, I kept my eyes focused on Him, feeling complete, whole, and at one with all. Suddenly the devotee next to me tapped me on the shoulder. I turned to her and she asked, "Why are you sitting there? He said, 'Go.'" Why, of course, He had. How could I have been so unaware? I am reminded now of a well known English bhajan which says, "I am in samadhi* when Swami is with me."

Whether my state could be called samadhi or not, it can certainly be called bliss.

Now that I had been brought back to the present time and place, however, I got up and stepped outside, checking to be sure that Raye saw me and would come also. The Seva Dals were instantly alert and brought the wheelchair for me. So, for the first time this trip, I was seated in the wheelchair at the foot of the ramp to the interview room, waiting for Swami to arrive from darshan. Raye was seated on the bench nearest the gate through which Swami would come.

When He came, He went straight to Raye and asked, "Where is your life?" Without a moment's hesitation, Raye pointed to me. Swami smiled and enthusiastically approved his answer. He said, "That's right! Wife is life!" Then He came to me. As He approached, He raised His right hand, and when He stopped in front of the wheelchair, He swung His hand down, hitting both knees with one swing, then He went back across and back again, feeding both knees and legs with His energy. Afterward, He looked down at me and said, "Now go up that ramp--fast!"

I went up the ramp--fast! I was the first one inside, so I sat on the floor as close as I could get to Swami's chair. While waiting for the others to come in, I pondered Swami's remarks to Raye at the beginning of each interview. Prior to the first interview, He had asked why he wasn't sitting with his wife since his wife was his life. Before the second interview, He had reminded him again that his wife was his life. This time He had turned the question around, asking where was his life. What was the teaching here? Kabir had once commented that when a wife adhered strictly to her dharma that the householder's life was the best training ground for spiritual development. I had just reached the conclusion that the teaching in it for me was that I must adhere strictly to my dharma, when Swami came in. He had to squeeze in between me and His chair in order to sit down.

After exchanging a few words with some of the others whom He had called, He turned to me, asking (I thought) "Where is happiness?" I replied, "Happiness is everywhere." But once more I had misunderstood His question. He had asked, "What is happiness?" So, He now said, "No, happiness is union with God." Immediately I realized that He was emphasizing the teaching He had been giving me when He said, "Very, very happy," in response to my tale of woe about how sick I had been. He knows that I am One with God the same as He knows Himself to be One with God. Understanding this Union, happiness is the only possible response to any occurrence, whatever we might call it humanly.

As in each of the first two interviews, He again asked, "How many kilos do you weigh?" This time, having been weighed several times in the hospital, I was able to answer the question as He asked it, and I replied, "One hundred ten, Swami." He accepted the answer. However, if He asks me again, I hope to remember to say, "The body weighs one hundred ten kilos, but I am not the body."

After further interaction with others in the group, He told Raye and me to go inside. With some assistance, I got up and went inside, seating myself again at Swami's feet. This time I had a few questions which I had been eagerly hoping to ask Swami, and I began as soon as He sat down.

"Swami, was it You who sent me the vibhuti in the hospital?" Even though I knew in my heart that it had to have been He, I wanted to have His confirmation before I wrote it as a fact. His reaction was instant. He sounded both surprised at the question and somewhat disappointed at me for asking it, saying "Don't you know? Didn't you know that I was there in that hospital room with you? I never left your side for a minute. I answered your prayer." I lowered my eyes, saying, "Yes, Swami, I felt Your presence there," but went on with my questioning for the sake of absolute accuracy.

"Did you cancel the cancer, Swami?" This time He responded even more vehemently than He had to the first question. He virtually shouted, "No cancer! No cancer! Cancer is cancelled!" His response gave me the greatest sense of peace that I had ever experienced. Not only by His words but also by the tone of His voice, I was assured that He would always be with me and would destroy any enemy which might attack.

Now I came to another question which I most urgently needed to ask. After Swami had told us that He would give us a place of our own in Brindavan, we had become aware of an apartment building which was being constructed adjacent to the ashram. The ground floor apartment which would best serve our needs was still available. Was this another instance in which we needed to recognize the "I" as ourselves and to take action, or were we to take Swami's word as we would any other human commitment? Having difficulty making this discrimination, I was delighted to have the chance to ask Swami directly. So, I said, "Swami, there is an available ground floor apartment adjacent to the ashram, should we buy it?" Again, He spoke in such a way as to leave us with no doubt. In a loud, firm voice, He replied, "No! Don't waste your money! I told you that I would give you a place of your own inside!"

Only one question remained. As both **Life Is a Game, Play It!** and **Life Is a Challenge, Meet It!** had been published by the Books and Publications Trust and their release was imminent, I asked Swami if I should bring the negatives for **Life Is a Dream, Realize It!** when I returned. He answered positively, adding that the new book should be published before we returned and that we should bring the negatives for it also.

When we returned to the outer room, Swami addressed the group and, referring to me, said, "She is a scholar." She has written four books. They are: **Life Is a Game, Play It!, Life Is a Challenge, Meet It!, Life Is a Dream, Realize It!, and Life Is Love, Enjoy It!**" I knew that there were some negative aspects to being called a scholar**, but I was delighted at His naming the four books in the order in which I had written them, despite the fact that He frequently uses a different order when He states the phrases in His teaching.

He had given the same loving care and attention to all of us in the interview, manifesting a watch for one, sizing a ring for another, and generally caring for His lambs with whatever individual attention was required to further each one's spiritual growth. At one point, as He was moving about the room, He turned to me and said very softly, "Form is One." This remark referred back to my saying in the first interview, "I so love to be with the Form, Swami." Now He was demanding that I go up one more step in my understanding and recognize that the Form is One. Like every good teacher, Swami has faith in His students' ability to learn more and more. But what a hard teaching! Form is One. I'll have to ponder that one for a while.

The time was drawing to an end. Swami signed a picture which a devotee had handed to me just before darshan that morning. It was of Swami in darshan near me, and it was the only thing I had with me that morning. It is now a treasured signed photo, just another tiny instance of the amazing grace which He showers on us all every day.

As we left the interview room, Swami standing at the door like the incredibly wonderful host that He is, I asked just one more question. "Swami, will we be able to return by Christmas?" "Yes, Christmas," He replied. "Very happy, very happy!"

* * * * * * * * *

**The term "samadhi" is generally identified with a temporary loss of consciousness, or even more—a temporary heightening of the consciousness. But we have to judge the state by the effect it has on the person and his attitude towards himself and others. "Samadhi" combines "sama" (equal) and "dhi" (intelligence), that* *is to say, intelligence grasping the fundamental equality of every being. Not only will all ideas of difference and distinction disappear, but even the idea of quality—heat and cold, grief and joy, good and bad—will disappear. When man reaches that state, the Lord is automatically born in his consciousness.*

The moment Krishna was born, the chains that bound his father fell off, the doors that had been bolted flew open, and the prison guards were immersed in the ocean of bliss so that they could not recognize any event or thing in the material world.

Sathya Sai Baba
Sathya Sai Speaks, Vol. X, Chap. 29

**When the mind is turned inwards, it looks only at the atma and does not look at the external surroundings. Therefore, when your mind is turned inwards, you will not notice the difference between pleasure and pain, between sorrow and happiness, or between heat and cold. In fact, the mind will not take note of any differences and disparities at all. It is the oneness of everything that you will be able to realize. When an individual is in a state of samadhi, he has nothing to do with the world although he is moving about in the world.*

Sathya Sai Baba
Summer Showers in Brindavan 1973, p. 71

A person who has mastered and lives the* ***Vedas *might be honored as a pundit. Another might be praised for his brilliant writings in both prose and verse. But if such scholars have neither purity of consciousness nor elevating ideals, their capacities will result in more harm than good. They will promote neither happiness of the people nor peace in society. They will pass through life without the awareness of its sanctity or sublimity.*

Sathya Sai Baba
Sathya Sai Speaks, Vol. X, Chap. 9

Hanuman had succeeded in coordinating the thought, the word, and the act. Therefore, he had the unique distinction of being great in physical strength, mental stability, and virtuous character. He shines as an invaluable gem among the personalities of the* ***Ramayana. *He was also a great scholar, who had mastered, of all things, the six schools of grammar! He knew the four* ***Vedas*** *and the six* ***Sastras.*** *The* ***Geetha*** *says that a scholar is one who sees the same Divine force motivating everyone. Hanuman was the very picture of humility, born out of genuine sincerity and wisdom.*

Sathya Sai Baba
Sathya Sai Speaks, Vol. X, Chap. 18

AMAZING GRACE

Amazing Grace, how sweet the sound
That saved a soul like me.
I once was lost, but now I'm found,
Was blind, but now I see.

'Twas Grace that taught my heart
to fear
And Grace my fears relieved.
How precious did that Grace appear
The hour I first believed.

When we've been there ten thousand
years,
Bright shining as the sun,
We've no less days to sing God's praise
Than when we first begun.

Through many trials, toils, and snares,
I have already come.
'Twas Grace that led me safe thus
far,
And Grace will lead me on.

Amazing Grace our Sai bestows.
His love no boundary knows.
Not one is lost, but all are freed
From sin, desire, and need.
--No more sin, desire, or need.

Chapter Twenty-Five

THE PROCESS OF DETACHMENT

Leaving Swami, after being with Him for four months--or even four days--is never easy, but perhaps we were able to detach from His physical presence a little more easily this time, knowing that we would be returning soon. Even though the human appearance was that we were separated from Him, He had made it abundantly clear that He was always with us, and evidences of His care were always there.

Our trip home is usually broken up by an overnight stay in Kuala Lumpur. A night spent in a comfortable hotel seems to alleviate the jet lag just a little bit. As our trip budget was almost entirely depleted by the extra expenses we had incurred, we considered foregoing the overnight rest, but finally decided that it would be better to be overdrawn than overtired. Thus we arrived in Kuala Lumpur and were assisted into the terminal by the ever-courteous airline personnel. As we reached the ground floor, our kind helper told us to wait just a moment and he would get a hotel voucher for us. Raye and I looked at each other in surprise. It was our understanding that we were to pay our own expenses at the hotel. A few minutes later, the gentleman returned with meal tickets and a hotel voucher, saying that our stay in Kuala Lumpur would be paid for by the airline. Just one more little evidence of Swami's grace as shown by the airline's dharmic management.

Our return to Los Angeles was somehow different this time. Always before it had been accompanied by a feeling of homecoming. This time it seemed more like a stopover on the way home. But there was much to be done. We had a house full of things to dispose of, many of which dated back forty or fifty years. This clearing out of old treasures with their memories would definitely be an exercise in detachment.

As the process began, I found that I did quite well most of the time. When I had things that could be used by friends, I was happy. When a cupboard became empty, I felt relieved and somehow lighter and freer. But there were times when I hit a snag. Occasionally a sense of loss or regret would occur over the most unlikely object. A dear little koala bear which had been sent by a devotee friend in Australia was very hard to part with. Funny, I hadn't had it very long--I hadn't known the person who sent it very well--what was the attachment? Pondering this, I realized that it was the love that had prompted the giving of the gift which was causing this attachment. Was I going to lose the love if I found another home for the gift? Certainly not! The mind can be demonic if we don't take time to uncover its tricks. The love would stay with me. It wouldn't even make my suitcase any heavier!

So, little by little, I released those things that needed to be released--those things which had no real substance anyway--and kept the things which were truly substantial. It was clear that I would never take any of this with me when I shed these old clothes that I call "my body," what difference did it make if they went a little sooner?

...man has to give up his pursuit of sensory objects if he seeks lasting peace and joy. Material wealth brings along with it not only joy but grief as well. Accumulation of riches, multiplication of wants, these lead only to alternation between joy and grief. Attachment is the root of both joy and grief; detachment is the savior. A millionaire pays income tax with tears in his eyes; the Headmaster joyfully gives up the furniture and laboratory appliances of his school when he is transferred to some other place. Why? Because the Headmaster knows that he is only the caretaker, not the owner. He is not attached to those articles; he knows they belong to the government. So, too, feel that your family, your house, your fields, your car, are all the Lord's property and that you are only the trustee; be ready to give them up without a murmur at a moment's notice.

*The sacred literature of our country, the **Vedas,** the **Sastras,** the **Ithihasas, Manusmrithi,** and the **Puranas** contain the drugs to cure attachment and endow you with the strength of detachment. Drugs available at other places, though they may be more pleasant, waste time and money and do not assuage pain. Renunciation does not mean that you should not value things; you may. You may even care for them. But always remember* *that they are transient, that the joy they give is temporal and temporary. This is to say, do not overvalue them. Know their real worth....*

It is difficult to put into practice even truths of which you are intellectually convinced. Look at Drona on the battlefield. When he heard that Aswatthama had been killed, he was so overcome with sorrow that he did not pause to consider where he was and for what end. Even if the news were true, he should not have laid down arms, forgetting the task upon which he had come to the field. It was the delusion that some people are nearer one than others which induced him to do so. That delusion was the reason for his discomfiture and death.

I would like to tell you that it is not what you hear that is beneficial but what you put into daily practice. Develop renunciation about your own needs and wishes. Examine each on the touchstone of essentiality. When you pile up things in your apartments, you only promote darkness and dust. So, also, do not store too many materials in your mind. Travel light. Have just enough to sustain life and maintain health. The dal must have just enough salt to make it relishing; adding too much will spoil it. Life becomes too difficult to bear if you put too much desire into it. Limit your desires to your capacity, and, even then, have only those that will grant lasting joy. Do not run after fashion and public approval and strain your resources beyond repair. Also, keep to your own dharma and the code of rules that regulate the stage of life you have reached.

Sathya Sai Baba
Sathya Sai Speaks, Vol. IV, Chap. 16

We did not have too much difficulty in regard to leaving our many good friends. Since all of our friends are Baba devotees, they will be coming to India to be with Swami, and we will have the opportunity to see them also. However, I did feel some concern about my daughter. She had on more than one occasion begged Raye not to let me follow my wish to live in India. Even though she lives in Iowa, and we see each other seldom, she could not quite accept the idea that I would be on the other side of the world from her.

However, after Swami had given His approval to our making the move, I wrote to her, sending her pictures of Swami speaking to me in darshan. That touched her heart. She wrote a beautiful letter in response, giving her permission and blessing for our move. She said that she could understand how wonderful it would be to be able to see your Master every day, and that she would not put any obstacle in my way of doing that. She will come to California to visit us before we leave, and our love will be in Iowa with her and her love will be in India with Raye and me.

That is another of Swami's most precious gifts to me--a loving and understanding daughter. And it may be that the highest expression of Mother Love is to give the grown child the opportunity to learn detachment, instilling the essential truth that God is closer than the human mother. (See **Sathya Sai Speaks, Vol. XI,** Chap. 39)

> *Human activity and worship depend upon the level of attainment you have reached, the particular stage of your life, as well as the human characteristics that rule you.... There is a way of life, a method of uplift, a path of progress distinct for every seeker, different from the paths of others. The True Guru knows which suits you best. It does not mean that the Guru is partial or prejudiced; it only means that he is kind and considerate, for he does not insist that all men wear the same straitjacket....*
>
> *The whole secret lies in detachment.... The mind must be unaffected by the experiences of success and failure, of gain and loss, of wellness and illness; it must be surrendered at the Feet of the Lord. Let His will prevail. What profit does your little will bring you? Just close your eyes for five minutes and think of the profit your efforts have won for you. One wish leads to another; one bond brings about ten others.... The Vedic injunction, given through the sages, is: Speak the Truth; walk in the path of virtue.... Truth will win, whatever*

*the obstacle; otherwise, the **Vedas** would not have commanded man to stick to it.*

Sathya Sai Baba
Sathya Sai Speaks, Vol. IV, Chap. 48

Don't Worry; Be Happy!

Don't worry; be happy; our Father loves us so.
Illusions are many, but underneath them all
There's one reality--that you and I are One--
That God is Love and Love is God and God and
man are One.

Chapter Twenty-Six

ENJOY IT ALL

It seems to me now that there are four stages of life. The first is ignorance of anything beyond the material world, the body, and the senses; that is, the state of bondage. The senses instill delusion, and man becomes the slave of the senses, not knowing himself nor God, but being hopelessly lost in a fog of sensual pleasures, desire, and attachment. However, since more grief than joy is engendered by attachment, eventually man begins to seek a way out of his misery. He asks, "Who am I? Why am I here? What is the purpose of life?"

When these questions are asked, Truth is always there to answer. Swami says, "Truth is more fundamental than the atom," and "Your Truth is in your own self." It is plain that we can never be separated from our own self; therefore, we can never be separated from Truth. But what is it that keeps us continually deluded and a slave to our desires?

The mind is the mischief-maker. Swami says, "It is the mind that reacts to external objects and events, pronouncing them good or bad; this is why it is essential to achieve control of the mind." He goes on to describe the nature of the mind:

> *The fulfillment of man's life on earth consists in filling himself with Love of God and transmuting that love into acts of service—service of man who is the embodiment of God. If*

man has no love in him, and if he does not share love with all beings, he is but a burden to the earth.

Make your emotions pure; make your mind strong to resist the force of ignorance and the wiles of the senses—then you are assured of peace and joy. You maintain health by physical exercise, so, too, you must maintain mental health (for the mind can lead you into bondage or liberation) by means of certain exercises.

For example, by means of pure food, the mind can be rendered pure and sharp; it can then cut through obstacles and temptations and rend the veil of misconception. You must also try to be constantly in a good environment, in good company, in a spiritual organization.

In a spiritual organization, members do not discuss what can be seen or heard, touched or tasted; they are interested in the investigation of the Unseen, the basic Truth beyond the senses (outer and inner), the processes by which the mind helps or hinders the individual's journey to God.

The mind is called a karana, an instrument. The senses are instruments which are used to contact nature and gather information about objects. Mind is the overall instrument. It is called the antahkarana, the inner instrument. Higher than the mind is the buddhi, the intellect, which analyzes and categorizes the impressions as gathered by the mind, through the senses. The buddhi is subordinate to the chitta, consciousness, and the ego or I-sense, which is fundamental to the individual. The mind has to be subordinate to the intellect, but usually it serves the senses, which are in reality only its servants. That is how the mind leads man into bondage....

But beyond the mind, beyond reason, consciousness, and the I-sense, is the Atma, the reality, the Cosmic I, or God. Rational knowledge, or knowledge accumulated by the exercise of the senses and stored and sifted by reason, is but illusory knowledge. It is worldly material knowledge, subject to correction or modification. The question arises: how can you be content, living in this illusory world, gathering and relying on this illusory knowledge? Realize the Person beyond all illusion, who is the Creator of this illusion, who is revealed in and through this illusion. Worldly knowledge is of the temporary, the particular, the finite, the individual; how can it reveal the Eternal, the Universal, the Infinite, the Absolute? The ***Vedas*** *give the answer.*

They ask us to analyze our dream-experience. Dreams are unreal; they are illusory. Yet for as long as we *are dreaming, the experience is real and valid. Often in these dreams, as a result of the illusory experience itself, awareness of such extreme is created through fear, horror, pain, or excitement, that the person dreaming awakens and the dream is destroyed. What has caused the awakening? The dream itself helped in the destruction of the dream. So, too, in this wakeful dream—in the illusory world where every waking experience is deemed true and valid—some experience, or the roar of the **Vedas** in the Divine Axioms which ring through the sacred texts, wakes man into the Higher Awareness.*

Sathya Sai Baba
Sathya Sai Speaks, Vol. VII, Chap. 63

Having been awakened from the illusory dream of life being limited to the mind and the senses, man begins his search for answers. Each one's search leads him ultimately to the Truth within himself, passing through various religions, philosophies, and practices on the way to that goal. Occasionally, hearing of the experiences that another has had along the path, one may receive inspiration and guidance which is also helpful to him. It was in this belief that I began writing this quartet of books twelve years ago.

My own journey to God began in earnest when I found Sathya Sai Baba. It was so wonderful! Life took on meaning. I found the answers for which I had been searching. Truth was beginning to unfold within me. As St. John described in the book of Revelation, the taste of Truth was so sweet as I began to take it in! Even though I knew the quotation well, somehow I never expected to go through the bitterness of digestion. ("Take it [Truth] and eat it up; and it shall make thy belly bitter, but it shall be in thy mouth sweet as honey.") However, some of the experiences which I have related in these pages have had some of that bitterness. Even the bitter experiences are blessings, though, because they dislodge the most stubborn of our mistaken, longheld beliefs.

Then can we still believe that Life is Love? Can we still enjoy it? I truly think that we can. With Swami's Grace, we will! Mrs. Eddy told Christian Scientists, "Do not murmur over Truth if you find its digestion bitter."

Our self-effort involves controlling the mind. Baba says, "Likes and dislikes depend on the mind, not on the matter." We can choose to dislike and be unhappy about any experience which comes our way. Or, we can choose to be grateful that "Whatever happens has to happen," and that everything happens for the purpose of bringing us home to God, to mergence in eternal Bliss. God is Good! That is the bottom line. And happiness is that state of mind which is unaffected by anything that happens, however it might be classified by human thinking. "God is beyond all notions of good and bad," Swami says, adding, "You are God, not this body."

The lessons which I have learned, during and after the difficult experiences which we have had recently, have been worth much more than the pain and suffering of the body and the mind which they entailed. As Paul told the Corinthians,

> "All things are for your sakes, that the abundant grace might through the thanksgiving of many redound to the glory of God. For which cause we faint not; but, though our outward man perish, yet the inward man is renewed day by day. For our light affliction, which is but for a moment, worketh for us a far more exceeding and eternal weight of glory; while we look not at the things which are seen, but at the things which are not seen. For the things which are seen are temporal, but the things which are not seen are eternal."

Holy Bible, II Corinthians 4:15-18

And our Swami, who is the Avatar to this age, bringing to us the ultimate Truth, has taken the Revelation of St. John one step further, adding the fourth stage which we may expect in our growth Spiritward.

1) We began in ignorance;

2) Sought Truth, finding it sweet at its first taste.

3) We continued through the stage of digestion, perhaps having some bitter experiences;

4) Now, if we are practicing what we have learned, we can expect the transformation to become evident. Our speech will become sweet with love for God and man, understanding the Oneness of All. Our looks will become sweet as the mind is no longer filled with desires and attachments.

Everything about us will be sweet, as we surrender everything to our Beloved Lord and completely identify ourselves with Divine Love.

Baba said it this way.

> *The experience while digesting [Truth] was bitter.... However, in due course, there was a great transformation in St. John. His speech acquired a unique sweetness. His looks were sweet. Everything about him became sweet. What does this mean? It signifies the truth that you should completely identify yourself with Divine Love, which you now seek from God. This love is not a purchasable commodity.*
>
> *Today devotion is treated as an exercise in shareholding, a kind of business partnership. But this is not right. The devotees should feel "Everything is Thine." It is only when there is such a feeling of total surrender that the nature of Divine Love can be comprehended.*

Sathya Sai Baba
Christmas Discourse, 1993

When we know all to be His, we can be happy. When we know that He and I (Form) is One, we can be happy. When we practise loving and serving our fellowman, we can be happy. When we know Love to be all there is, we can be happy. When we know that Life is Love, we can enjoy it! Be happy, dear readers. Your bliss is His food.

BIBLIOGRAPHY

Goel, B. S., **Third Eye and Kundalini**, Third Eye Foundation of India, 1985.

Narasimha, H. H., **Sri Sai Baba's Charters and Sayings**, India.

Sanella, Lee M.D., **The Kundalini Experience**, Integral Publishing, 1992.

Sathya Sai Baba, **Geetha Vahini**, Sri Sathya Sai Books and Publications Trust, Prasanthi Nilayam.

Sathya Sai Speaks, Vols. I-XI, Sri Sathya Sai Books and Publications Trust, Prasanthi Nilayam.

St. John, Gloria, **The Way Home**, Coral Leaf Press, 1992.